THE TOP CONSULTANT

THE TOP CONSULTANT

DEVELOPING YOUR SKILLS
FOR GREATER EFFECTIVENESS

4TH EDITION

CALVERT MARKHAM

RECOMMENDED BY
INSTITUTE OF DIRECTORS

**KOGAN
PAGE**

London and Philadelphia

Publishers' note

Both masculine and feminine pronouns have been used in this book. This stems from a desire to avoid ugly and cumbersome language, and no discrimination, prejudice or bias is intended.

Every possible effort has been made to ensure that the information contained in this book is accurate at the time of going to press, and the publisher and author cannot accept responsibility for any errors or omissions, however caused. No responsibility for loss or damage occasioned to any person acting, or refraining from action, as a result of the material in this publication can be accepted by the editor, the publisher or the author.

First published in 1993
Second edition 1994
Third edition 1998
Third revised edition 2001
Fourth edition 2004
Reprinted 2008

Kogan Page Limited
120 Pentonville Road
London N1 9JN
United Kingdom
www.koganpage.com

Kogan Page US
525 South 4th Street, #241
Philadelphia PA 19147
USA

ISBN 10: 0 7494 4253 0
ISBN 13: 978 0 7494 4253 8

British Library Cataloguing-in-Publication Data

A CIP record for this book is available from the British Library.

Library of Congress Cataloging-in-Publication Data

Markham, Calvert
  The top consultant: developing your skills for greater effectiveness/
  Calvert Markham. -- 4th ed.
    p. cm.
  Includes blibliographical references and index
  ISBN 0-7494-4253-0
  1. Business consultants. 2. Career development. I. Title.
HD69.C6M373 2004
001'.023'73--dc22
                                                    2004014338

Typeset by Datamatics Technologies Ltd, Mumbai, India
Printed and bound in Great Britain by Biddles Ltd, King's Lynn, Norfolk

Contents

Preface

'Management Consultant' was an unusual occupation when I started my career but nowadays consultancy is a commonplace activity. Many will see a spell as a consultant as an essential ingredient of a well-rounded CV, while others, like me, make a career of it.

There are two main drivers to the growth in consultancy:

1. the propensity of organizations increasingly to outsource more core activities, to which consultancy firms have responded with an expanding range of services;

2. organizations whose main business is not consultancy, which have sought revenue and/or competitive advantage by selling their know-how – that is, offering consultancy – perhaps evolving from an internal consultancy activity.

Consultancy involves skills in delivering services to clients and in running a consultancy business and this book addresses both these topics. Career progression in consultancy leads to commercial and business management responsibilities and these are therefore likely to be undertaken by more experienced consultants in larger practices, while sole practitioners need to consider them from the outset.

Latterly, internal support functions (such as HR and IT) have also been encouraged to take on consultancy roles. Line managers, too, increasingly need to introduce discontinuous change, demanding a measure of consultancy skills.

Whatever your role, I hope that you will find ideas and techniques in this book that will enable you to develop your performance and become a 'Top Consultant'.

Acknowledgements

Consultancy is a skill, honed through practice and experience. My thanks therefore go to my clients with whom I have been able to work on consultancy projects and, more latterly, in designing and delivering training programmes in consultancy. The experiences shared by other consultants whom I have met in the course of this work have also been enriching; the training has been a two-way street!

I have completely revised, updated and restructured the book in the current edition. When it was first published, I gave my thanks to my wife and son for their forbearance during the periods of seclusion required by an author. Now, more than 10 years on, I have my son Charles to thank for the rigorous proofreading he has done of the draft. I haven't accepted all his suggestions so any remaining errors are entirely my responsibility!

1

The nature of consultancy

One hundred years ago, the management consultancy industry did not exist; now, consultancy is globally a multi-billion dollar industry, covering many service lines in addition to management. In recent years, consultancy firms have expanded to include thousands of consultants handling large-scale projects and process outsourcing activities, while at the same time there is a horde of sole practitioners and small firms delivering more modest consultancy services to their clients. So, what is this consultancy business? In this chapter we will consider what consultancy is, why consultants are engaged, the nature of the organizations delivering consultancy services, and the skills required of consultants.

WHAT IS CONSULTANCY?

One of my first assignments as a management consultant was with one of the London teaching hospitals. I heard that a colleague was a patient in one of the wards and I wanted to know which one, so I phoned the appropriate department. Information was given only reluctantly over the phone, until I was asked who I was. 'I'm a consultant and she's a member of my firm', I replied, honestly. There was a sound of clicking heels as the person at the other end of the phone came to attention – and I got the information I wanted immediately. 'Consultant' and 'firm' had quite different (and more potent) meanings in a hospital.

The term 'consultant' is now used for a variety of occupations; as well as the senior doctor and the management consultant, it is used to describe anybody who is providing knowledge-based services to an organization on a contractual basis. So 'consultant' can also include solicitor, accountant, architect, engineer or, indeed, any profession.

A simple definition of consultancy is 'delivering specialist skills from outside the organization'. Key concepts in this definition are: 1) *specialist skills* – the assumption is that the consultant has specific skills, in demand and valued by the client organization, and it is for this reason that the individual consultant has been engaged; 2) *outside the organization* – the consultant is usually from another organization or, if an internal consultant, from a different department within the organization. Occasionally someone may be called on to exercise a consultancy role within their own business unit, in which case they will need to adopt the behaviours of an internal consultant.

Arguably, any provider of professional services might be regarded as a consultant; indeed, the methods of winning business and handling clients will have much in common. But the matters on which management consultants are engaged involve helping organizations define and implement their development agendas. The development agenda is not only about doing new things, but also about doing existing things better.

The nature of management consultancy interventions has evolved, as shown in Figure 1.1. As the diagram shows, consultants can be involved at a number of levels:

1. *Providing advice.* This work might answer a question such as: 'What is the reward package needed to attract a good marketing manager?'

2. *Project design* goes a step further, answering questions such as: 'How do we ensure that our reward packages remain competitive?'

3. *Implementation* goes a step still further: 'Install a new reward system for this business that gives better value for money.'

4. *Functional management* takes on running a complete function: 'Please run our reward system on our behalf.'

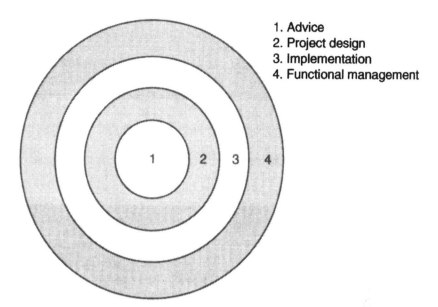

1. Advice
2. Project design
3. Implementation
4. Functional management

Figure 1.1 Evolution of activities in a consultancy practice

Each stage represents an increased level of outsourcing and a larger 'footprint' for the consultancy practice in the client organization. For example, an HR manager may be charged with managing a company reward system and decide to initiate a project to ensure that the reward remains competitive, enlisting the help of consultants to design this (level 2), which he or she then implements (level 3). These steps therefore represent an evolving degree towards 'buy' in terms of strategic 'make or buy' decisions.

WHY USE CONSULTANTS?

All organizations have suppliers – of utilities, raw materials and so on. Organizations need to decide what they should source internally and what they should buy in the 'make or buy' decision.

The structure of business has changed radically over the last 30 years: whereas large corporations would have had teams of in-house specialists to help with projects as and when required, the consequence of successive cost-cutting exercises has been that many specialist departments have closed. Specialist expertise is now externally resourced – not only in consultancy and other professions, but also in many other areas – for example, office cleaning, running canteens and security. Activities that are not vital to the core of the business are subcontracted. Charles Handy (1989), in his book *The Age of Unreason*, sees this trend developing and greatly affecting the nature and structure of organizations.

So, the principle of using specialist outsiders is established. The next question is: On what activities should they be engaged? The obvious areas are where organizations do not have the quantity or quality of resources to achieve the desired results. A simple analogy: you want to replace the central heating system in your house; if you do not know how to do this, you will probably engage a plumber to do it for you. Or, you may be able to do it, but have insufficient time to do so, in which case you would again subcontract the work.

There are three other factors that organizations may also take into consideration when deciding whether to subcontract:

- *Objectivity.* Will insiders bring the independence and freshness of view that an outsider would bring?

- *Risk.* Bringing in outside experts should mitigate the risks of the project failing (and, if you are cynical, will provide an obvious scapegoat if it does!).

- *Learning.* There are two questions for clients to consider:

    - How will our organizational knowledge be increased as a result of using consultants?

    - What opportunities for learning will be lost by engaging outside consultants?

Taking the central heating analogy above, for example, you may wish to work alongside the plumber if you want to learn how to install central heating systems for yourself in future.

These factors are also relevant to the use of internal consultants. The value of establishing an internal consultancy practice is that it allows the development of a centre of excellence in an area of specialist activity that would not be economically viable if diffused throughout an organization. Moreover, leading-edge practice is not

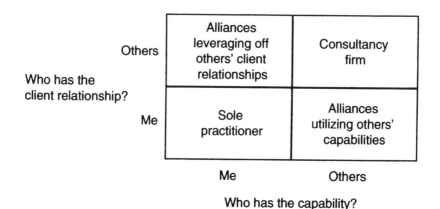

Figure 1.2   Evolution of activities in a consultancy practice

always available from external consultancies. Organizations may be able to acquire learning and capability in areas relevant to their business more easily than consultants. In many situations a joint client–consultant team therefore can be very effective.

THE NATURE OF CONSULTANCY PRACTICES

There are clear benefits in consultants associating. Quite apart from the economies of scale in sharing administrative overheads, there is far more likelihood that the right blend of skills to address clients' issues will be available from a group of consultants than from a sole practitioner.

There are two major tasks in consultancy, both of which take time: acquiring engagements, and executing them. Figure 1.2 shows how consultants can leverage the two resources required to carry these out – their network of client contacts and their specialist skills.

Associations of consultants can vary from a loose network through to a formally constituted practice. The latter will have a well-developed infrastructure with consultants trained in using shared procedures working with clients. In recent years large consultancy practices have flourished, developing on a global level and taking on massive projects, either by themselves or as part of a consortium, the latter often involving partners from quite different kinds of business.

THE ROLE OF THE CONSULTANT

The role of the consultant within the consultancy practice has also evolved over the last 30 years:

- To the early/mid-1970s. The consultant was the conduit through which the specialist knowledge of a practice was transmitted. Management consultancies' 'products' would consist of well-tried services or methodologies; the theory and practice of their introduction would be incorporated in manuals.

- Early 1970s–mid-1980s. The consultant as 'management mercenary'. The consultant would be a generalist, perhaps with an MBA (Master of Business Administration) or some similar qualification. His or her role would be that of a gun for hire – a bright trouble-shooter who could take a new problem and resolve it from first principles. Previous experience was not essential; what was offered was a general skill.

- Early 1980s–mid-1990s. The consultant as specialist. The consultant is hired because of the relevance of his or her skills to the problem in hand. Previous experience and personal expertise are important, but must be complemented with a capability to deliver specialist skills in a client environment.

- Currently. The consultant may be a stand-alone resource hired to identify and/or address organizational issues, or could be part of a team involving other specialists reconfiguring entire functions or systems for an organization.

Of course, these phases not only overlap but also are not exclusive. Plainly there were specialists operating before the mid-1970s and there are consultancy practices that currently offer proprietary approaches. In branches of consultancy outside management consultancy – IT (information technology) consultancy, for example – experience may also be different. There are now signs that the wheel has come full circle. Major consultancies nowadays offer proven methodologies to their clients to address their problems. Consultants are recruited and trained in operating these methodologies.

A feature of the evolution described above is a trend from hiring not only a consultancy per se but also assessing the people in the consultancy. Clients have become more discerning and are not only interested in the reputation of the practice but also in the quality of the consultants put forward. It is therefore worth considering the provenance of people who become management consultants.

WHAT SORT OF PEOPLE BECOME CONSULTANTS?

Many people become consultants, having previously worked in specialist line positions. Indeed, management consultancies often draw their recruits from this source and develop them by training and supervision in the skills required of a consultant.

Other specialists have chosen to become freelance consultants because they have been made redundant or have taken early retirement. For many in this group, the notion of consultancy is not about the professional skills involved but more about their commercial relationship with those who are paying them – they are no longer employees, but self-employed contractors. Some will continue to confine their role to specialist subcontractor, while others will develop consultancy skills.

For those in a consultancy practice, there is a choice of role. Consultants can be simply the trained providers of a proprietary product or promoted as experts in their own right. Each approach has advantages and disadvantages. The practice with proprietary consultancy approaches will presumably market them as such, so a newcomer to the market has therefore not only to develop a new approach, and to prove that it is workable, but also to challenge the brand of the established provider. By contrast, if the consultancy product is vested in the skills of an individual consultant, it is easy for the specialist to leave this employment and take his or her skills – and possibly clients – to another employer, or set up his or her own consultancy business. This is of course how some of even the most venerable of the consultancies in the United Kingdom were started.

THE RELATIONSHIP BETWEEN THE PRACTICE AND THE CLIENT

At one extreme the relationship between the consultancy practice and the client is arm's-length; the consultancy is employed on a one-off basis to meet a specific need that the client is unable to meet from its own resources. At the other extreme there is an almost symbiotic relationship; the consultancy has been selected not only because of the value it can add to the client's business, but also because they feel comfortable doing business together – there is a good cultural match. With the evolution mentioned earlier, so too has the typical relationship between consultancy practice and client developed, from the arm's-length sale to the alliance based on a long-term mutual benefit.

Not all relationships between consultancies and their clients will be this close, of course; at the start, many will be on an arm's-length basis, anyway. The important point is that there has been a change in mind-set; a consultancy is not engaged in just a sale: it is developing an alliance. Long-term considerations apply, rather than just those relating to the immediate transaction with the client.

Again, the growth of the consultancy business means that it is quite possible that a senior executive commissioning a consultancy project may have had a period of experience as a consultant (or will have worked with consultants before) and will be familiar with the techniques of selling and operating consultancy assignments. Clients have matured in their evaluation of the consultancy offering. This means that there is now a larger measure of equality between consultants and their clients.

CONSULTANCY SKILLS

There are three components to consultancy skills:

- The body of knowledge, skills and experience that the consultant has on offer. This might be civil engineering, tax law, software applications or whatever the consultant is expert in.

- Experience or knowledge of the application of the specialist skill to a specific area. This might be, for example, an industrial sector, a geographical area, or a particular type of problem.

- Consultancy skills, which enable the consultant to deliver his or her expertise within the client environment.

These three components are like the legs of a three-legged stool: all have to be present if a consultant is to carry out the role effectively. If one leg is missing, the stool is at best wobbly and at worst falls over. This book concentrates on the third component – the skills required to engage in consultancy, which are necessary irrespective of the specialist expertise of the individual or the area of its application. The skills can be divided into two: 1) those relating to business aspects of consultancy: product development and marketing; the sales process and how to manage it; commercial aspects of dealing with clients; and managing the business as a whole; 2) those needed to conduct these tasks well: how to sell; problem solving; operating consultancy projects; and managing client relationships throughout.

There is overlap between all these topics. But the message that the reader should take away is that it is not sufficient simply to have knowledge to be effective as a consultant: there are real skills needed as well – and these are the basis of this book.

2

Managing a consultancy business

As with any other business, a management consultancy has to be managed and, if only in the long term, the quality of management will influence the performance of the business. It is not the purpose of this book to rehearse the general principles of management; it is useful, however, to consider the critical elements that need to be managed. A useful general model of key elements in a consultancy practice is illustrated in Figure 2.1.

The model in Figure 2.1 shows that the function of a consultancy organization is to enable consultants and clients to add value to each other through harnessing the leadership, infrastructure and intellectual property of the consultancy practice. Within the infrastructure will be the critical processes involved in defining, selling and delivering consultancy services – the core of the business.

The tasks and skills involved in consultants engaging effectively with clients are dealt with in the following chapters, while leadership and intellectual property are dealt with in the following sections in this chapter.

LEADERSHIP IN A CONSULTANCY PRACTICE

I seem to remember from the days when I was taught corporate strategy that the first question to ask when fashioning a strategy is: 'What business are we in?' Perhaps strategic thinking has moved on since then but it is a good question to ask of a consultancy business. Large consultancy practices have taken to adding a strapline to all their publicity material as an answer to this question. This is

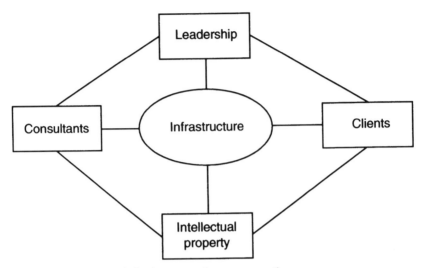

Figure 2.1   A model of a consultancy practice

usually something to the effect of 'Helping our clients to become more successful' or similar. But how is this to be done?

Consultancies add value to their clients through the medium of their consultants. Figure 2.2 shows a model of a consulting practice, expressed as exchanges of value between consultancy firm, consultant and client.

For the purposes of business management, we need to consider the exchanges of value involving the consultancy firm at both operational and strategic levels. The key question for any consultancy firm is: 'What do we as a firm add to the transaction between consultant and client?'

At its simplest, consultancy is simply brokerage: the consultancy practice introduces its clients to specialists who have the technical skills needed to carry out the work required. The consultant has the benefit of carrying his or her employer's franchise – they are being employed as consultants at least partly because they bear the imprimatur of their employer. The client has the reassurance of the reputation of the practice underwriting the work of the individual consultants. The practice makes a profit on the difference between what they charge the client and what they pay the consultant.

The thought will occur eventually to both client and consultant that it might be to the advantage of both to cut out the intermediary

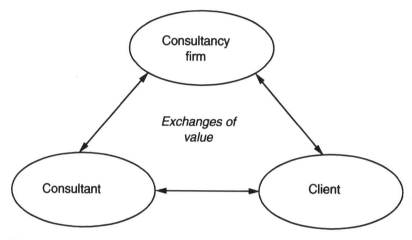

Figure 2.2   An added value model of consultancy

– the consultancy firm. A sole practitioner is the result of this thinking taken to its logical conclusion. None the less, there is a role for a broker between clients and consultants but this is more often the function of networks or associations than that of a consultancy practice. So, a consultancy firm has to offer something more in the long term.

INTELLECTUAL PROPERTY IN A CONSULTANCY PRACTICE

Know-how (knowledge, skill and experience) is the principal resource that the consultancy firm offers its clients. Technology transfer is the firm's ability to apply these to the benefit of its clients.

The reason an organization might turn to a consultancy firm for help is for the resources that it offers. A particular firm may be employed for a number of reasons, including:

- It has knowledge that the organization does not have.

- Although the organization has the knowledge, it does not have as much experience in applying it as the consultancy firm does, or needs the objective view of an outsider.

- Although the organization has the knowledge and experience, it does not have them sufficiently available to engage in the project.

A consultancy firm therefore needs to ensure that it has the resources (in terms of the skill mix and volume) required to meet the needs of organizations in its marketplace. These needs are, of course, changing and so a firm should aim to have the knowledge and experience required to meet these changing needs through selective recruitment and training.

Several points merit consideration concerning technology transfer:

- A firm should operate not only in responsive mode; it should alert its clients to opportunities and needs, of which the clients may otherwise be unaware. To this end, a firm should be 'horizon scanning' continually. Sometimes a large practice might have an advisory board or panel to help with this, made up partly of outsiders, such as academics, business people, politicians and civil servants. They would alert the firm to trends, opportunities and innovations, which might affect the firm's clientele and its own business. Even without an advisory panel, the consultancy business manager should make sure that horizon scanning is done regularly.

- The firm should be able to put together its knowledge and experience in ways that are attractive to its clients (this is product and market development: see Chapter 3). This does not mean that consultancy offerings are unilaterally the work of the consultancy firm; they may result from strategic alliances with other firms or individuals. Anyhow, they should be put forward as offering synergy between firm and client and, perhaps, developed jointly with the client. There has to be some basis for a discussion to start, however, and the firm should take the initiative on this.

- The firm must deliver its knowledge and experience to its clients effectively. This means that individual consultants must be able to work in a client environment (see below under 'Attracting and retaining talented people' regarding personal development). Collectively, the firm must offer operating methodologies that ease technology transfer and the ability to put together teams of consultants who can work together effectively.

This last point is important. The consultancy firm's know-how consists not only of the knowledge that it deploys to the benefit of its clients, but also skills in deploying that knowledge. These skills result from experience – experience that belongs to individual consultants within the firm. A key process, therefore, is capturing individual learning and making it corporately available – often embodied in standard procedures or guidelines. Knowledge acquisition and diffusion processes are hence an important component of corporate performance.

These take time. At the simplest level, they require consultant teams to undertake project reviews and to capture and disseminate the lessons learned. Unless this is enforced as a formal discipline, consultants often prefer to move on to the next project with no pause for reflection, and the opportunity for organizational learning is lost.

It is only in recent years that knowledge management has gained widespread attention, but this is perhaps the most helpful paradigm for a consultancy firm. Processes of management should enhance this acquisition and distribution of know-how to the benefit of consultants and clients.

MANAGING CONSULTANTS

The 'make or buy' decision

As with any other business, a consultancy is faced with a 'make or buy' decision. The major elements of expense are likely to be salaries and office accommodation. There will be other expenses, some of which are directly recoverable from clients, and the development and maintenance of a support infrastructure, but salaries are likely to be the biggest element of expense. The costs in a consultancy practice are therefore mainly fixed. (This was vividly illustrated in one consultancy firm that made about 10 per cent profit; 'Our profit each week is earned only on Friday afternoon', I was told.)

If costs are to be made more variable, therefore, the consultancy firm has to consider whether to employ people or take them on only on a project by project basis, as subcontractors or associates.

The greater expense arising is compensated by the fact that in recessionary times subcontractors can be laid off, while the core team of consultants remains intact. Other considerations in using subcontractors include:

- How should they be badged? Should the client be told that they are using subcontractors?

- Will key learning and experience of value to the consultancy practice be lost by using subcontractors?

- How will subcontractors be integrated into the project team? If the consultancy operates a particular methodology, will the subcontractor be able to operate within it? Does the consultancy add value to the subcontractor's services or is it simply acting as a broker?

This last question relates to the level of investment a consultancy practice makes in each of its subcontractors. If they are trained in the consultancy's methodology, this represents an expense and a possible dilution of the practice's differentiation through its methodology. What some firms do is to keep in contact with 'graduates' – consultants who, having been trained by the firm, have left to start up their own practices. They therefore form a pool of trained resources that can be called on when required.

Remuneration

The cost of consultants is also related to remuneration policy. Consultancy practices are not exempt from the general rules governing remuneration, that is, that the fairness of a consultant's remuneration package will be judged by external comparisons (what they might earn if they performed a similar job elsewhere) and internal comparisons (their remuneration in relation to that of others in the practice).

Where consultancy differs from many other employments is in the career patterns of employees. Often, people who enter consultancy plan to spend only part of their careers within the profession, say four to five years, before moving on to further employment as executives in businesses other than consultancy. There is thus a higher staff turnover rate at junior levels in a practice than at senior levels, the latter being populated primarily by those who have chosen to make their career in consultancy. This pattern of staff turnover has the advantages that it enables new people with fresh ideas to be brought into the firm and those who leave will do so with (we hope) a fund of goodwill towards their former employer, and become clients in their new role.

What this means is that there are two classes of employee in a consultancy practice: those who are doing a job as a stepping stone to something else and those who see consultancy as a career. Most people entering consultancy start in the first category and there is thus a transition point when they move into the second. It is important that both the consultancy firm and the individual consultant share the same view of which category the consultant is in. Misapprehensions on either side will result in disappointment. What some consultancy firms do, therefore, is to have career reviews with consultants at significant points in their careers at – say – intervals of three to five years. These reviews elicit the individual's career aspirations and potential and plan how they can be best met within the practice, or whether a move outside would be better.

The relevance of this to pay is that it points to different pay policies for the two categories. The pay package for the former will consist of primarily short-term elements, for example, basic pay, profit sharing bonus, company car. The pay package for the latter will, in addition, have long-term elements, such as pension and stock options or another form of capital appreciation plan. This distinction is perhaps most recognizable in firms that are partnerships, where being made a partner of the firm has traditionally been an indicator of being offered a long-term career (although this has not always been the case in recent years).

At an operational level, pay is significant because, as a large fixed expense, it can create problems in cash flow. The firm has to pay the consultant before the client pays the firm. It can also create problems in volume sensitivity. If fee revenue goes down, the firm still has to pay the same salary bill. Actions that can be taken to deal with these are as follows:

- Defer payment by paying salaries later in arrears. This will provide a (one-off) reduction in cash requirements.

- Defer payment by paying a low monthly salary, but adding an annual supplement (a bonus) that brings it up to market rate.

- Relate the size of the bonus to business profitability. This will make salary a partially variable cost; when profits are low, bonus will be smaller, thereby reducing employee costs.

Obviously any action on pay must take into account market practice and the probable response of the consultants to the changes proposed.

Attracting and retaining talented people

In the same way that they compete for clients, consultancy practices compete for talent. Often they are seeking recruits with similar backgrounds, abilities and experience and, for the most part, talented people are in short supply. Consultancy practices have therefore to consider how they market themselves to prospective recruits, and how to continue to offer an attractive prospectus to their own consultants. Employment conditions have to be right, but beyond this a key element of the prospectus for existing and prospective employees is the opportunities for personal growth – the value added to individual employability by working in a particular practice.

Consultants wish to practise, maintain, refresh and increase their technical skills. This they can achieve in part by working on consultancy assignments. They will also need to keep their technical skills up to date by attending appropriate courses and conferences, reading specialist literature and so on. Besides technical skills, however, they need to know how to deliver their skills in a client environment and how to effect change in organizations as a consultant.

Many people learn their technical skills as an employee and have learned how to discharge them as such. Working in a client environment as a consultant is different. Many topics covered in this book, for example, would be irrelevant to the specialist employee. The commercial environment in which the consultant works, the needs for marketing, selling and client care, the importance of project management, are all peculiarly relevant to a consultant.

A management consultant is also an agent of change. If consultants are to fulfil this role effectively, they must understand the pathology of organizations so that they can interact with them to achieve change.

There are therefore specific consultancy skills to be added to the specialist expertise of a new consultant. To a large extent, consultancy is a craft: skill has to develop through practical experience, as much as, if not more than, through formal training. Every consultancy business can therefore provide at least the practical part of the training component. Whether it provides formal training may be a function of size. The reasons for training consultants are:

● Training may be needed to bring new staff to the standards of operating required.

● Training may be needed to maintain and develop the skills of experienced consultants.

● New skills can be imparted and developed by training.

● Offering structured approaches to personal development may help the practice to attract and retain good quality staff.

Given that consultancy is a craft skill, the apprenticeship model is a helpful one in developing skills on the job. Skilled consultants can supervise or act as mentors to those less experienced. In the early stages of a consultant's career, he or she may keep a log of activities in which they have been engaged. Their project work could then be selected to fill in gaps in experience, extending their skills, or improving in areas of weakness.

The individual consultant gains much by working on client assignments. Personal development occurs not only through the development activities organized by the consultancy firm, but also through the consultant's assignment experience.

A benefit of working for a consultancy practice is that it enables you to work at the periphery of your expertise. Under the umbrella of the firm, you may work in a project team in which you can learn as much, if not more, than you contribute. Personal development is therefore helped at an operational level by assigning consultants to projects that help them to grow. This is something more difficult to do as a sole practitioner, where clients employ you in the centre of your expertise, and there is less scope for working in areas where you have little previous experience.

ORGANIZATION STRUCTURE WITHIN A CONSULTANCY PRACTICE

Like other industries, many forms of organization have been tried out in consultancy:

- industry focused groups;
- consultants grouped by specialization;
- regional groups, concentrated by geography;
- a combination of some or all of the above.

There is no one right answer. Form should follow function, and so organization structure should be an element of infrastructure that improves the ability of a consultancy practice to enhance its key processes.

Tasks and roles in a consultancy practice

There are a variety of tasks in all management consultancies, which can be subsumed in the following roles:

- practice manager;
- account manager (salesperson);
- bid manager;
- project manager;
- resource manager;
- auditor;
- operating consultant.

In a small practice, these roles may be carried out by a single individual; in a large one, they may be spread among several people. It is not unusual for someone to be engaged in more than one role. For example, an individual could be taking the role of an account manager or as project manager in the sales process. Subsequently he or she might conduct the project as the operating consultant. An explanation of each of the above roles is set out below.

Practice manager

The role of practice manager is to manage the business of the consultancy practice, or a part thereof. This is a general management role, with responsibility for producing a profit stream.

The survival and profitability of a consultancy's business are superordinate objectives. The practice manager therefore usually has the greatest seniority within a consultancy unit. At an operational level he or she will be setting priorities and targets and resolving questions of conflict between others in the consultancy unit, for example, over competition for resources. The practice manager therefore sets the (internal) commercial environment in which consultancy projects are conducted. The practice manager will also be responsible for setting strategy for his or her unit, within that for the practice as a whole.

Account manager

As consultants derive much of their revenue from past clients, the role of the account manager is to maintain links with (specified) past and present clients, and may also be responsible for winning business from new ones. The account manager may have a specialization as a consultant but frequently this may not be relevant to the client's current needs. Other consultants will therefore be engaged in projects for the account manager's clients. But when the project is complete, the project team will move on to other assignments for other clients and the account manager will be left to maintain the client relationship. In this respect, the account manager is a bridge between consultancy and client and the various sales are the vehicles passing over the bridge. Even when there is no traffic, the bridge exists; if there is no bridge, there can be no traffic. So, the relationship must be maintained, even when there are no current projects. Thus, while the practice manager sets the commercial context for the project from the firm's point of view, the account manager will be managing the context of the project from a client relationship point of view.

Bid manager

A bid, or proposal, for a piece of consultancy work might simply involve a short letter. If the project is to be of any size, however, it will involve devoting some time and effort to preparing a proposal, which is a project in itself.

In some practices, this is formally recognized by the appointment of a bid manager. The task of the bid manager is to define the terms of reference for the project, to prescribe the methodology, to assess the resources required to carry it out and to prepare a costing of them. It may also involve assessing the risks associated with the project and, where these are felt to be substantial, seeking authority to proceed with putting in the bid.

Usually the account manager or the project manager who is going to work on the project will take this role. Occasionally, however, there may be people whose specialization is preparing proposals on specific topics.

Project manager

The job of the consultancy project manager is to meet the project objectives, within the allocated resources, while maintaining good relationships with client staff. It is sensible on any operating consultancy project to appoint one person who is responsible for its delivery. The project manager may report to the account manager on project matters, in that the account manager is overseeing the ongoing relationship with the client and the commercial context of the project. If there is only one consultant involved with the project, he or she has to take the role of project manager.

Resource manager

It is unusual for consultants to be permanently allocated to a single account. The task of resource management is to deploy consultants among accounts and projects, and to ensure that their utilization is optimized. Consultants might be allocated to groups for the purposes of resource management according to location or specialization. Resource managers may also act as 'product champions', with the aim of promoting their specialist services among the internal connectors – account managers – and thence to the consultancy's client base.

Auditor

The job of auditor is sometimes called quality manager or quality assurance director. The purpose of the role is to monitor projects against quality standards and to design and carry out procedures to ensure that suitable quality standards are established and maintained.

Over the last decade it has become clear that quality is not simply a policing function but something that provides a real commercial and competitive advantage. The purpose of the auditor is to provide someone outside the sales and operating teams involved with the sale or delivery of a particular project, who can helpfully comment on how well these tasks are being carried out.

An auditor might carry out inspections of bids or projects to see that they conform to good practice. Inspections can be conducted after a bid is won or lost, at the conclusion of a project or some time after the end of a project. The auditor can also be a source of counsel and advice during the project. This does not have to be a full-time role; for example, a consultant in Division A of a business can act as auditor for projects in Division B and vice versa.

Operating consultant

This is the default role and those individuals filling the previous six roles will probably also operate on assignments. It is common practice that even the most senior individual within a firm will do work with a client, although practice management and account management tasks may consume most of his or her time. Operating consultants may also have responsibilities for some sales aspects.

When you enter a consultancy practice, you normally do so as an operating consultant. The other roles above are taken on with increasing experience. What this means in practice is that there is a decoupling of rank and role – performance of a particular role does not imply seniority (except that of the practice manager). Thus, for example, A might supervise B on one activity, whereas on another, B might supervise A.

3

Product definition and marketing in consultancy

Figure 2.1 in the previous chapter shows the key elements to be managed in consultancy. We noted that the critical processes within the infrastructure were selling and delivering consultancy projects; these have to be in the context of client engagement, which forms the subject matter for the rest of this book.

Consultancy activities are frequently referred to as services but herein we will be referring to them as *products*. Consultancy products are the means by which value is added to the client and so we start with the notion of product definition. Product definition and market definition go hand in hand, so this chapter continues with some thoughts about marketing consultancy products. In this text, marketing is distinguished from selling as relating to clients in general, while selling is to specific clients.

Ralph Waldo Emerson wrote: 'If a man... make a better mousetrap than his neighbour, tho' he build his house in the woods, the world will make a beaten path to his door.' But your efforts will avail you naught if the world doesn't recognize the need for a mousetrap, or doesn't know you've built a better one, or has no idea where your door is.

So, what is the consultancy 'mousetrap' (product) and how can you market and sell it? These topics are addressed using the model shown in Figure 3.1. This shows the hierarchy of matters to be considered:

Figure 3.1 Business development in a consultancy firm

- *Product-market definition* is the foundation of the business.

- *Account management* describes how the consultancy relates to its clients. Account management is ongoing, whether or not the consultancy is currently doing work for that client.

- *Sales management* is about managing the sales process and sales in aggregate whereas, by contrast...

- *Selling* is about conducting a single sales transaction.

PRODUCT DEFINITION

The basic activities involved in consultancy (the topics covered in this book) vary very little. To this extent, consultancy products offer the same old wine in new bottles. Skills in issue analysis, data collection, diagnosis and creating change within a client environment, will be common to many consultancy offerings. In the same way that a cabinetmaker may change his or her designs to suit current fashion but continue to use the same skills, management consultants focus their perennial skills on organizational matters of current concern – for example, on cost reduction in a recession, on growth strategies in a boom.

Product definition in consultancy is best described as the packaging of experience, which is then communicated by marketing and selling. Experience may be imported with a new recruit, or it may derive from experience in carrying out a consultancy assignment for a client; either way, if it is to be sold, it has then to be packaged into a consultancy service – something that can be replicated.

Wherever it is positioned, the consultancy service has to be communicable. In the same way that a cabinetmaker would find it easier to describe his or her craft in terms of the products he or she makes, so too consultants need to describe their services in terms of the processes used and the benefits arising from them. For example, in the mid-1980s a consultancy employed an expert in knowledge engineering for the first time – the only specialist of his kind within the firm. He had no previous experience of consultancy and the consultancy was not quite clear what he had on offer. The results were that his specialist experience was never sold because it had not been packaged as a communicable offering.

There are other similarities between the consultant and the cabinetmaker. The job that the cabinetmaker does, for example, depends on the customer's specification. Similarly, the job done by the consultant consists of harnessing his or her skills to meet the requirements of the terms of reference as agreed. A difference, however, is that whereas the cabinetmaker can point to other items of furniture he or she may have created, it is less easy for the consultant to do so because the product is intangible. This is commonly dealt with by using references from previous clients or citing previous experiences, which can refer to the activities involved and results achieved.

Even when a consultancy has had some success in carrying out assignments in a particular area, there is some merit in 'packaging' this experience. If a consultancy had developed an approach that helped employers to reduce levels of absenteeism by half, this would be of great interest to large organizations. Few buyers, however, would have sufficient confidence to commission a consultancy project simply because the consultants asserted this was possible. Buyers would want to know how these results were achieved; they might want to talk to other clients for whom the consultants had done a similar job in the past. All these are steps that serve to reduce the sense of risk and increase confidence. Ultimately, all that a client gets when he or she buys a consultancy assignment is a promise. Packaging a consultancy product increases the client's confidence that the promise can be kept. A packaged consultancy product consists of:

- *A name.* At best, this can become a brand (for example, 'the X job evaluation system') or at the least make reference to it simple (for example, 'activity-based costing').

- *An explanation* of its purpose and the methodology used in carrying it out.

- Descriptions of *situations* in which it might be of use and the benefits of so doing.

- Information on *previous applications* of the technique and the benefits obtained.

Often a consultancy will publish a brochure describing the product; in this case, to the above list would be added information to meet the criteria set out in the section on 'Marketing objectives' below. Finally, if consultancy salespeople are to promote the product, they will need 'golden nuggets': stories illustrating the benefits of introducing the consultancy product, together with some indication of the likely costs of consultancy help. I have often found it useful to test out new product concepts with friendly clients. Although not necessarily prospective purchasers of the product, they can be an invaluable source of feedback from a client's point of view.

There are some who, with some justification, claim that consultancy is a fashion business. The list of 'fashionable' products is extensive: process re-engineering, quality circles, overhead value analysis, management by objectives, total quality management, were all popular in their time. And all have delivered value to their users, but may now be out of fashion. There is therefore a need for consultancies – as with any other business – to maintain a flow of new products to meet the needs of their customers. Fashion may not be rational; but ignoring fashion in consultancy is like telling a couturier that the only purpose of clothing is to keep the rain off! And, to be fair, the delivery of 'old fashioned' products can be improved with increasing experience, and then repackaged and relaunched.

Joint ventures and strategic alliances

In many respects, consultancy product development has characteristics similar to cookery. A skilled chef, working from a small range of ingredients, can create a wide variety of appealing dishes. In a

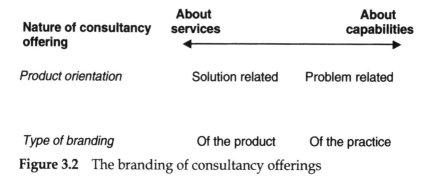

Figure 3.2 The branding of consultancy offerings

similar way, consultants put together capabilities to create offerings attractive to clients. In Chapter 1, we saw that consultants associate for this purpose, but often the capabilities required do not lie within a single firm of consultants and so they engage in joint ventures. 'Capabilities' in this context may not simply mean technical abilities – it might mean access to a market, or a depth of resource. For example, in entering a foreign market a consultancy might seek a joint venture partner.

Although it may not be involved in a strategic alliance, a large consultancy will need to become accustomed to forming consortia to bid for major projects. Resources required for projects in these circumstances will be drawn from subcontractors and joint ventures, working within a framework of the consultancy's own methodologies.

Having defined the consultancy product, the firm now needs to decide how best to project it to its target market sectors.

Branding in consultancy

Within any business, you need to decide what you want to be famous for. Branding is the aggregation of these attributes. Figure 3.2 shows how consultancy offerings relate to the type of branding.

At one end of the spectrum in Figure 3.2 the offering is shown as being about services. These are methodologies that are predefined, although their application may be tailored to the needs of a client. A good example is a proprietary job evaluation system, whose principles of operation and method of introduction to a business will be standardized, although the details will be varied according to each client's requirements. Such an offering is solution related – that is, the problem has already been defined. Under these circumstances, the product should be branded – for example, the XYZ job evaluation system.

At the other end of the spectrum, the offering is shown as being about capabilities. Practices in this position may offer an embracing methodology for working with clients in dealing with problems of a particular type. This is an approach to conducting assignments rather than being related to a particular area of service. In these circumstances, Figure 3.2 suggests that the practice should be branded.

The difference between product and practice branding can be illustrated by an example from retail. Imagine that your aunt has been invited to a special event for which she needs a new outfit. She might say, 'I've no idea what to wear; I'll go along to Harrods to see if they have any ideas.' This is the equivalent of practice branding; she is going to Harrods because of its reputation, but with no specific purchase in mind. Alternatively, she might say, 'I think I need a beige dress in classic style – I'll visit Oxford Street to see if I can find one.' This case is equivalent to product branding – she knows what she wants, and has to find someone to provide it.

In the context of consultancy, a firm may promote itself as 'specialists in managing change'. They have not said what kind of change they are involved in, and so are seeking to brand their practice. By contrast, another consultancy firm may offer a service called 'Office Move', dealing with all aspects of helping a business relocate. Businesses will be more attracted to 'Office Move' if they have decided that relocation is what is required.

There is some strategic advantage in branding the firm rather than the service. The prospective client may not be able to see the link between the service and the problem with which he or she is confronted (although the consultancy's promotional literature will seek to make this clear!). Unless the client can be persuaded to see the service as addressing the problem, then they may reject the consultancies offering these, instead preferring to go straight to those practices that specialize in the sort of problems confronting them. The providers of solutions are like – say – a Chinese restaurant: if you want Chinese food, the ideal place to go, but not otherwise.

A further advantage for firms branded as dealing with problems is that they will usually have to start with some diagnosis. This positions them well for follow-on work in creating and implementing solutions to the problems, as well as extending the size of their market. By contrast, the client will have done much of the diagnosis for those offering solutions. For example, if approaching a recruitment consultant, a client will have already diagnosed the need for a recruit.

Given the advantages for the branded firm, consultancy firms will often have the strategic aim of moving from product branding to practice branding. The risk for those who are the providers of solutions only in doing this is that the results of their studies will always be the same – whatever the starting conditions, the same solution is prescribed. Like Henry Ford, they offer 'any colour, as long as it's black'.

MARKETING CONSULTANCY

A simple distinction between marketing and selling consultancy services is that in selling you have a specific client in view; by contrast, marketing is to a specific sector – that is, many prospective clients. Note that I have taken a limited definition of marketing as essentially the promotion of a consultancy firm and its services. Marketing purists would no doubt argue for a broader definition, emphasizing the need for the business to be marketing oriented. Consultancy, however, is by nature a peculiarly market oriented business. Most people of any seniority in a firm – if not most consultants – have daily contact with their customers; few businesses outside the professions can boast as much contact. Moreover, every professional is called on to promote, if not sell, his or her firm's services, which again requires a strong market orientation.

The aim of marketing is to:

- generate a demand for and raise awareness of a consultancy product;

- help to generate or identify good prospects;

- position the practice as a provider of (the defined) consultancy services.

Marketing in a consultancy business therefore consists largely of promotional activities. There are, of course, professional restrictions on the methods by which consultants may promote themselves. For example, the Institute of Management Consultancy has laid down general guidelines for its members, but does not forbid cold calling, provided the guidelines are followed. Other professional institutes may, however, have more severe restrictions on promotional activities, which should of course be observed by their members.

Marketing objectives

There are five criteria that have to be satisfied before a client will open a dialogue on working together with a consultant. They are:

1. The client has to recognize that a problem exists.

2. The client must believe that the problem is sufficiently important to merit attention.

3. The client must believe that the problem can be resolved.

4. The client must decide that outside help is required to resolve the problem.

5. The client must decide that your practice is worth considering for this work.

(There will be further hurdles for the consultancy to surmount before receiving an invitation to tender, which must be dealt with as part of the sales process.)

The objectives of marketing should be to help to see that these five main criteria are satisfied. The consultancy that is attempting to market a new service may have to start at stage 1. At the other extreme, stages 1 to 4 may have been completed by the client without any prompting from a consultancy practice; it merely remains for the client to select a consultancy to work on the project.

Set out below are the activities you can undertake that will help to satisfy these criteria:

- *The client has to recognize that a problem exists.* To go to a client with the offer of a service to solve a problem that it does not recognize as such stands as much chance of success as a plumber who wants to repair your central heating when nothing is wrong. Clients recognize problems when:

- there is a problem or opportunity where previously none was thought to exist. Often these arise from change in the environment. For example, concern with corporate social responsibility; business process outsourcing; managing diversity; and knowledge management all represent features that have changed in the environment, which have led to consultancy opportunities. The job of the marketing consultant in these circumstances is to draw the attention of the client to the problem.

- the problem is generally recognized, but the client did not know it occurred in his or her organization. This is when data feedback is often used by consultants – for example, a general survey of some feature of a business sector so that clients can compare the performance of their own organization with those of others. Examples are myriad in personnel matters (pay, benefits, labour, turnover, etc) where there are hosts of surveys to which client organizations can subscribe.

● *The client has to believe that the problem is important.* Organizations are rife with problems. Many of the problems are liveable with or they eventually go away. No organization can afford to be problem free – there is a point of diminishing returns below which it is not worth tackling a problem. The way the consultancy markets in this respect is to show how the prospective returns are higher than the client originally thought.

Sometimes consultancies undertake a free survey to see whether the problem merits attention and, if so, what the likely return will be. For example, a consultancy that specializes in managing utility consumption (electricity, water, etc) might see whether any worthwhile reduction in consumption could be achieved by using their own special techniques.

● *The client must believe that the problem can be resolved.* There is the apocryphal story of the dictator who had two trays on his desk, one marked 'problems that time alone will solve', the other

Benefits of outside consultants	Benefits of internal staff
Objective	Know the internal politics
Provide an additional resource	Have to be paid anyhow
Experienced at dealing with this type of project	Experienced at dealing with this organization
Can change consultant personnel if client not satisfied	High incentive to please this client (employer!)

Figure 3.3 Relative benefits of using outside consultants and internal staff

marked 'problems that time alone has solved'. It is hard to imagine such a non-interventionist dictator! In organizations, most people have plenty to do so do not want to waste their time attempting to resolve insoluble problems.

The task in marketing consultancy here is confidence building. If someone comes to you and says, 'I have a piece of kit that, attached to your car, will double your mileage per gallon of petrol', you might be sceptical. If you were to be assured by other users whose opinions you trusted that this was the case, then you might buy the kit. A reputation for success helps enormously.

- *The client must want outside help.* Much though it might go against the consultant's grain, organizations can solve their problems for themselves. Sometimes the competition for a consultant lies with the client's own staff rather than another consultancy. Figure 3.3 sets out some benefits of each.

Of course, these are not exclusive benefits. A consultancy may know a long-established client very well; alternatively, an internal member of staff may be very expert at dealing with the type of problem to be resolved. The job of consultants in marketing themselves at this point is to show how well equipped they are to address this type of problem, which is the purpose of promotional material.

- *The client must seek your help.* Clients will seek your help only if they know it is available. The purpose of marketing activity is to maintain awareness of your services among key people through promotional activities.

Who to market to

Research has shown that consultants get only 10–20 per cent of their work through sales promotion; the remainder comes from past clients and referrals. Promotion is vital, however, as a flow of new clients is required to maintain a consultancy business, let alone grow it. This is because there is usually some client loss – a client may go out of business, or choose to use a competitor, or may even have no problems left you can help with! So sales promotion is directed at prospective users of a consultancy's services.

Referrals – introductions and leads – come from connectors. Some professions are very accustomed to using connectors – for example, accountants cultivate bankers to get introductions to the bankers' clients, and there can be a flow in the other direction. Connectors for consultants depend on the nature of the specialization. Typically, referrals come from:

- existing or past clients;

- personal contacts;

- other consultancies (where not in competition);

- professional associations;

- other professional advisers.

In marketing to these, a consultancy aims to create a network. A strong network is necessary for all consultancies, whether a sole practitioner or a firm of more than a thousand professionals. Often, newcomers to consultancy underestimate the value of a good network. Junior consultants forget that they should cultivate their own networks as much as their more senior colleagues. In particular, they are well-positioned to identify and network with 'rising stars' in the client organizations with which they have worked.

Some two-thirds or more of a consultancy's business comes directly from past clients, and so they are obvious targets for receiving promotional material for new services. The advantages for a client in using the same consultancy for more than one assignment are that:

- they will have established an effective modus operandi for working together;

- the client will be confident in the consultancy;

- the consultancy will have learned about the client and the client's business.

Sometimes these factors will outweigh other considerations; once (when working as a sole practitioner), a client said to me of a new piece of work he asked me to do, 'I realize that this is not at the centre of your expertise, but I think you can do a good job for us. You know us and we know you, which is far more important.' (Which is also very gratifying, provided you can do the job!) So, existing clients should be a fruitful source of new business, by selling them additional services.

In large consultancies this presents a further need for marketing; no single individual can be in contact with all clients and know all the consultancy's services. There will be consultants who have account management responsibilities who themselves are specialists. They need to be informed of the other services the consultancy has on offer, and so the process of internal marketing has to be conducted in large practices. Account managers are internal connectors to the consultancy's clients, and so the provider of a specialist skill needs to promote it to these connectors as much as externally. Indeed, some commentators have estimated that in a large consultancy as much effort goes into internal marketing as external.

There remains the question of who to target as new clients. A useful technique here is to profile existing purchasers of your services and identify other organizations that have similar characteristics. These might be defined in terms of size, business sector, current circumstances or predicaments and so on. You then need to find a point of entry to the new prospective client. Again, you need to know who the typical purchasers of your services might be and then direct your promotional activities towards them. This is not necessarily a sure-fire method, however. Some years ago, a colleague remarked that she had been in contact with a target client organization and been told that there was no need for our services. In fact, our firm was already working extensively with this client! Two lessons emerge: 1) 'No' is not necessarily a final answer; 2) make sure you organize your selling so that you are not wasting promotional effort trying to win current clients!

PROMOTIONAL ACTIVITIES

Promotional activities can relate to the practice, the service, or the individual consultant. Practices promote themselves through advertising and sponsorship. Some larger ones have even gone to the considerable expense of using TV advertising. The aim here is to promote general capability rather than a specific service. This is particularly appropriate for large practices with a wide range of services. Some make use of promotional films, which they can show to prospective new clients, again with the aim of promoting the strength of the practice. This is corporate advertising – something that large organizations in other sectors have practised for years.

The methods by which practices promote their services among prospective and existing clients include:

- brochures and other promotional publications;

- house magazines or journals;

- articles in newspapers and magazines;

- carrying out, or sponsoring, research into a topic of interest, and making this available as a report;

- conferences, seminars, meetings, workshops, etc;

- entertainment – lunches, attendance at sporting occasions or other events.

The ways in which individuals in practices promote their services – or those of the practice – include:

- writing articles for newspapers and other periodicals or publishing books;

- appearances on TV or radio;

- membership of national or local bodies – professional associations, business or other societies.

The combination of these activities with networking can enable an individual consultant to become part of the client community he or she serves. It can then be perfectly natural for organizations to turn to this particular consultant and his or her firm for help when needed.

A Web site is also an essential marketing tool. It can be used to provide up to date information about the consultancy practice and its services, while its presence on suitable search engines can generate sales enquiries. It allows prospective clients an easy way of getting information about your business while, more importantly, the lack of a Web site would detract from your image.

These methods used to promote individuals and services can also be used to promote the practice as a whole.

4

The consultancy sales process

If you are sick and want treatment, you must go to a doctor. If you run a company, you are required to have an auditor. If you have legal problems, you need to consult a lawyer. Nobody has to have a management consultant. Consultants must therefore sell their services actively if they are to survive.

Simple arithmetic shows the commercial imperative to sell in a consultancy practice. Assume you have a medium-sized firm with 25 consultants with a basic pay, on average, of £40,000 per annum. Assume that fully absorbed on-costs and overheads are as much again as their salaries. The annual expenses of that consultancy will be £2 million. The fee income has to be £8,000 per working day just to cover costs. Sales of consultancy work obviously have to equal this if the firm is to break even.

It is a fortunate business that can generate sales at this level without any selling effort. Selling has to be active. If professionals are to be able to pursue their calling, there has to be an economic base sufficient to support them. The same applies to internal consultants. Although they may be 'free of charge', they receive a salary and incur other costs; they too have to justify their existence commercially.

How to manage selling is an issue for a practice with any more than a few professionals in it. There has to be some coordination through an organization structure, systems and procedures. Key to managing selling is recognizing that time is a consultant's stock in trade. If selling can be done more efficiently, hence requiring less time, a consultancy has competitive advantage.

A simple example illustrates this. Imagine that a one-person consultancy practice has 180 days available for work each year, after allocating time to holidays, training and administration. The consultant has set a revenue target of £75,000 for the year. If his or her sales ratio is 50 per cent, this means that he or she has to spend one day selling to generate two days' work. (This selling time would include pursuing unsuccessful prospects, as well as successful sales.) This means that he or she has to spend 60 days selling to generate 120 days' work. To reach his or her revenue target, his or her fee rate has to be (£75,000/120 =) £625 per day. If, however, he or she were a more successful salesperson with a sales ratio of 20 per cent, he or she would generate five days of sales for each day spent selling. In the consultant's year of 180 days, therefore, he or she would spend 30 days selling and 150 days operating. The consultant would therefore need to charge only £500 per day to reach the target revenue. Alternatively, were the consultant to charge the same as he or she would need to if he or she were less effective (that is, £625 per day), his or her annual income would be £93,750 or 25 per cent more. The reason, therefore, for being concerned with selling performance is to optimize this sales ratio.

THE CONSULTANCY SALES PROCESS

Product-market definition was dealt with in Chapter 3; but three other elements shown in Figure 3.1 (account management, sales management and selling) relate to selling to specific clients. Each of these depends on an understanding of the tasks involved in selling consultancy – the consultancy sales process.

The overall consultancy sales process is illustrated in Figure 4.1. Although a continuum of activity, it can be broken down into four main steps:

1. *Relationship development.* At the outset, a consultancy firm and prospective client may have no contact history or knowledge of each other. A relationship between consultancy and client has to be established before any sale can be developed.

2. *Prospection.* In the same way that gold prospectors pan for valuable nuggets, the next stage of the sales process is to find opportunities for consultancy and client to work together.

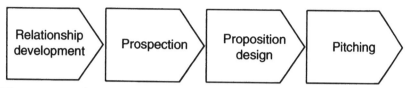

Figure 4.1 The consultancy sales process

3. *Developing the proposition.* Having found an area in which you might work together, the next step is to refine exactly what is going to be done. The consultancy may have a standard approach, but even in these cases, it must be tailored to meet the clients' specific needs.

4. *Pitching for the sale.* Having developed the proposition, it must be put over to the client in a compelling way.

Each of these is described in the following sections together with the critical factors influencing the performance of each.

RELATIONSHIP DEVELOPMENT

The sales processes involved in developing relationships with new and existing clients are known as hunting and farming respectively. Traditionally, hunters go out to find their quarry – departing from their home territory to wherever their quarry might be found. In like manner, the hunter-salesperson goes out beyond the existing client base to find new clients. By contrast, farmers stay on their homeland and use that to produce the food required; the farmer-salesperson produces new sales from an existing client base. Both hunting and farming are necessary, but – like their rural analogies – salespeople often have a preference and aptitude for one rather than the other.

The hunting process starts with *suspects* – those organizations that might need your consultancy services. If yours is a large consultancy, then all organizations might be suspects for the full range of your services. (Size of client organization is not necessarily a limit; I have worked for one of the largest corporations in the world in the same year that I also worked for an organization of only six people.) Such a large number of suspects is not helpful, and so it is best to look at them according to consultancy product.

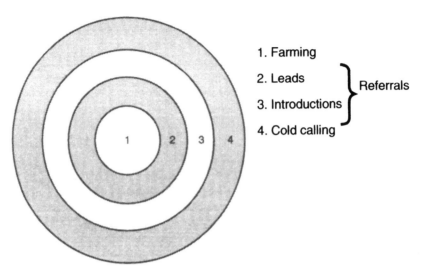

1. Farming
2. Leads ⎫
3. Introductions ⎬ Referrals
4. Cold calling ⎭

Figure 4.2 Developing relationships with new clients

The suspects might also be limited by market segmentation (for example, geography or industrial sector). From this long list of suspects you would select a shorter list of companies to approach – that is, *prospects*. These might be selected against criteria such as: 1) *a need for your service* – this might be general (for example, organizations are usually interested in worthwhile ideas for increasing performance) or event driven (for example, a company that has just made a new acquisition, or expanded into a new market); 2) *ease of access* – for example, you might choose to avoid companies that you know have a good relationship with one of your competitors who can supply the same consultancy services that you are trying to sell.

The next stage is to warm up the prospect so that they will agree to a meeting. This is a limited objective – that is, the approach is not to get the prospect to buy, but to secure the meeting – or to disqualify the organization as a prospect (see 'Qualification' in Chapter 5). The purpose of the meeting is to start building a relationship, and initiate the prospection process.

Figure 4.2 shows a model of hunting as a sort of target: the closer to the bull's-eye, the better the chances of success.

At the centre is shown farming; the link between hunting and farming is described below. Moving out from the bull's-eye are

	Existing	New
New to client	Cross selling	Hunting
Already bought	Maintaining awareness, selling on	Penetration

Service

Point of entry

Figure 4.3   Developing relationships with existing clients

shown leads and introductions. Both are kinds of referral via a connector. An introduction is to a client who might need your consultancy services. A lead is more than an introduction, in that the connector has seen an immediate requirement for the type of consultancy that you might offer.

Cold calling is the least fruitful of hunting activities as, in the words of one salesperson, 'You have to kiss a lot of frogs before you find a prince.' Cold calling with a telephone call out of the blue is least likely to work; 'warming up' clients beforehand is important so that they will be more receptive to that telephone call when it does come.

Farming is about developing relationships with existing clients. Figure 4.3 illustrates how this can be done.

A small organization may have only one purchaser of consultancy, but large ones have many. You may therefore seek new points of entry to existing clients. Similarly, you may try to sell services other than those being purchased already.

You need first to ensure that existing clients continue to use your practice to supply services as in the past. For example, a consultant in logistics would want to secure all consultancy work in this area from an existing client. If the client gave an assignment to a competitor, this would place the consultant's business under threat. So, you have to nurture existing clients so that your firm is the one that comes to mind when new opportunities arise for services that they have used in the past. This is about prospection.

Selling new services to an existing point of entry is called cross selling; establishing new points of entry with an existing client is penetration. If the salesperson is seeking to sell new services to a new point of entry, this is an activity similar to hunting, when you can get warm leads and introductions from one part of the organization to another.

Extrinsic and intrinsic selling

Imagine that you are moving house and you have a solicitor who is carrying out the conveyancing for you. At your final meeting with her, you remark that you will need to install a new central heating system in your house. Your solicitor then says, 'Oh, I can do that for you – I practise plumbing as well as law.' Now, it may be that your solicitor is the best and cheapest plumber to do this job, but you would need some convincing to accept her in this role. If she was to persuade you to consider her services, she would have to engage in *extrinsic selling*.

Extrinsic selling legitimizes the seller as a provider of a product or service. In the example above, the solicitor has to convince you that she is indeed a bona fide plumber before you would even start to discuss the work that you need doing. So extrinsic selling is persuading the prospective client that your consultancy practice is worth doing business with in the first place. By contrast, *intrinsic selling* is persuading the client of the merit of a particular proposition. Intrinsic selling will not be successful unless the extrinsic sales process has been completed, and completing the extrinsic sales process does not imply success in completing the intrinsic one. Continuing the example above, even if your solicitor does convince you that she can install your new heating system, you might seek quotations from other plumbers to make sure that her quotation is competitive and, if it isn't, you would choose another. Likewise, you will not work – say – with an insurance broker unless you are convinced that he or she will probably give you the service you want (the extrinsic process). On the other hand, you will not necessarily accept every suggestion he or she makes concerning the insurance policies you might invest in (the intrinsic process).

So, every sale consists of these two stages of extrinsic followed by intrinsic selling. Given the importance of managing time effectively in selling, then the less time that has to be spent on extrinsic selling, the more that can be spent on the intrinsic stage – making specific sales.

Marketing and promotion help the extrinsic sales process by developing a brand. The value of a brand is that it helps with extrinsic selling. If your consultancy practice is well known for its skill in introducing production control systems, say, then less effort is required to legitimize your consultancy offering in this area to a specific client. On the other hand, the same consultancy would have greater difficulty in selling assignments in – say – marketing, unless it was equally well known in its target market for this.

Note that in hunting, there has to be considerable extrinsic selling activity before you can engage in intrinsic selling. This is in marked contrast to the farming selling process because less effort is required in selling extrinsically to existing clients – they have already accepted your bona fides as a consultant. It is for this reason that consultants sell mainly to their existing client base. From the client's point of view too, there are advantages in dealing with the same consultant. It takes time to educate a consultant into the ways of a client's business. Dealing with a consultant used in the past avoids this time and cost.

It is worth noting that some extrinsic selling is required when seeking to sell new products or services to existing clients. This is vividly exemplified by IT hardware suppliers in the early 1990s. Faced with increasing competition and diminishing margins in their traditional markets, they enlarged their services to include consultancy. This presented a challenge to their sales forces. Say the names of any hardware supplier to a client and they would think of it as a hardware supplier; there was no need to legitimize it as such. When it came to their services as consultants, however, salespeople had for the first time to engage much more in extrinsic selling to persuade their clients to accept them as bona fide consultants.

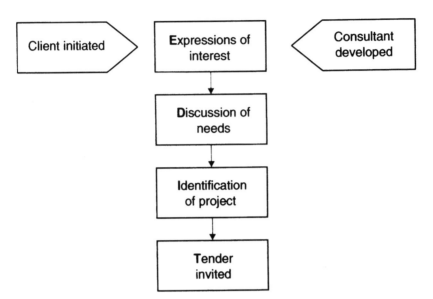

Figure 4.4 Prospection: The EDIT process

PROSPECTION

Figure 4.4 shows the prospection process. It involves mainly intrinsic selling if the consultancy practice is already legitimized as a provider of consultancy services, and a relationship has been formed with the prospective client. Otherwise, extrinsic selling is needed to position the consultancy and its offerings.

The easiest form of selling is where a client contacts you with a consultancy opportunity and asks for help. Clients will initiate contact only if they have some idea of the services and capabilities you have on offer, so raising and maintaining prospective clients' awareness of them is important. This is the task of promotional marketing, which is dealt with in Chapter 3.

The other (and more usual) method of prospection shown in Figure 4.4 is for the consultancy to be proactive by taking the initiative to develop sales. Strictly speaking, it should not be an option – a consultancy should be proactive anyhow. An opportunity can be developed by the consultancy when:

● there is an event of some significance for the client (for example, an announcement of business expansion, the loss of a key customer);

- there is a major change in the client's market sector – for example, new regulatory or environmental restrictions;

- you have a new service that could be of interest to the client;

- there is significant development among the client's competitors, which could result in a loss of competitive position;

- you have a strong view about an operational or strategic aspect of the client's business, and want to draw the client's attention to this.

On this last point it is worth emphasizing that I do believe that consultants can be advocates. It is in our interests to have successful clients – a consultancy firm will not flourish if its clients go out of business. If, therefore, as a consultant you can see an opportunity for a client to develop its business performance, then you should make representations to it about it. Indeed, the account management process in some practices has been formalized with respect to creating opportunities, rather than leaving it to happenstance. Someone in the consultancy account team will have the responsibility for looking ahead at the future needs of the client and making plans for how these are to be met, where appropriate, by providing consultancy support. (This activity is explained in more detail in Chapter 9.)

The 'EDIT' process illustrated in Figure 4.4 shows the progress towards an invitation to tender (ITT) or request for proposal (RFP). The four stages can be thought of as a funnel, as each does not automatically lead to the next. For example:

- Although the prospect may be interested, there is no immediate need for any activity in this area.

- Discussion of needs shows that no external support is required.

- The identification of the project shows that it lies outside the capabilities of your practice.

Only once these hurdles have been surmounted will you receive an invitation to tender.

DEVELOPING THE PROPOSITION

Consultancy is one of the least tangible products, and there is therefore considerable freedom to tune the proposition – the content and commercial aspects of project design – to meet the needs of the client. Contrast selling consultancy with the circumstances of someone selling chairs. They have only those chairs available from the factory to sell. Admittedly, they will probably be available in a variety of colours and styles, but if the customer wants something the factory doesn't make, then the salesperson is unlikely to make the sale.

The same is true, of course, for the consultant salesperson: if you cannot supply what the customer wants, then you will not make a sale. But selling consultancy involves the process of product specification. The consultant salesperson and the client work together to define the 'product' that the client is to buy. If this process is conducted well enough, then the consultancy will have created a proposition extremely attractive to the client. There is far more flexibility of design in consultancy than chairs, but to design an attractive proposition, you have to be able to identify what the critical features are for the client.

Critical features of a proposition

There are two aspects to a proposition: 1) *its content* – the definition of the nature of the project, and the contribution the consultancy is going to make, usually embodied in *terms of reference*; 2) its *commercial context* – relating to fees, expenses and other matters, usually embodied in *terms of business*.

Terms of business and terms of reference are dealt with at length in Chapters 7 and 8 respectively. In some major practices, different sales people deal with these two aspects separately. There are thus many potential features of propositions that need to be clarified during the sales process. The question is, which of these is critical? Features that might be critical could be:

- a particular consultant undertakes the job personally;
- the sponsor's position is enhanced;
- the project commences on Monday;
- the consultant introduces a new technology to the factory;
- the price is less than £50,000.

Clients give you a lot of information when raising objections. For example, questions such as:

- 'Do you have sufficient international experience?'
- 'Will you be able to complete the project in three months' time?'
- 'Do you understand our industry/culture?'
- 'Aren't you expensive?'

All give you useful information about features the client possibly considers important. You have, of course, to check whether these are serious questions, or simply incidental, during sales conversations (see the next chapter).

Further information will emerge during negotiation. Negotiation takes place when two parties have decided, or are close to deciding, that they want to do business together. At its most basic it consists of bargaining or trading, but at its best it consists of the two parties working together to refine a proposition so that it has more benefits for both.

When selecting consultants, clients who opt for a more formal process of selection may well have a 'scoring' system for assessing the relative merits of competitive proposals. It is useful to know what this is so that you can fashion an optimal proposition. Of course, there will be 'soft' measures as well. Recently I heard of a major buyer of consultancy that had rejected the 'best' proposal in favour of the 'second best', as the client buying team believed they could work better with the latter. Effective proposition design will not therefore automatically win sales, but it is a source of competitive advantage or disadvantage, and therefore has to be done well.

PITCHING FOR THE SALE

Your approach in pitching your proposition should be tailored to the buying process used by the client. You need to know how the buying decision is to be taken and the factors on which it is to be made. People who haven't met you will judge you only by your proposal; a presentation to an audience of decision-makers or influencers can help in building their confidence and reducing their sense of uncertainty.

Preparing a proposal

Whatever the selling or buying process being conducted, it is good practice to submit a written proposal, so that both you and the client have shared expectations of what is to be done. The function of the proposal may vary from being simply a record of what has already been orally agreed, to being the document on which the client is to make the buying decision. Some proposals may need to set out the rationale for carrying out the project in the first place (that is, the need for it and the benefits of proceeding). This is required when, for example, the client or the client's colleagues need to be reassured of the value of the project. If this is not required, then you need only to describe how you will meet the needs defined by the client and the reasons why your consultancy practice is particularly well suited so to do.

In taking the decision on what to include in your proposal, you need to consider the probable audience. What can they be safely assumed to know already? If in doubt, it is probably better to include explanatory material rather than leave it out. Ideally, the proposal should serve to confirm that which has already been discussed, but it should also bring some added value to the client.

Some years ago some associates and I were commissioning a piece of consultancy, and our experience is instructive. We interviewed four firms. With one, the meeting was curtailed; the consultant made some disparaging remarks about a couple of our competitors. My associate asked for us to be excused for a moment. Outside the meeting he said, 'We can't possibly use him. What if he were to make similar remarks about us?' So, we found an excuse to end the meeting.

A second consultant came from a large firm. Being ourselves a small firm, we had an uncomfortable (and possibly unfounded) feeling that we would not be treated with great importance because of our size. We were left with two contenders, both of whom we invited to put in proposals. One firm (Firm A), although we were not very taken with them at the outset, conducted a very good sales meeting; by the end, they were front-runners. Then we received their proposals.

Firm A sent in a proposal that simply confirmed the assignment. It seemed very much like a boilerplate job – that is, a standard proposal that had received some limited tailoring to meet our requirements. By contrast the other firm in the running – Firm B – produced a thoughtful proposal that really added value. It showed an appreciation of our circumstances, and contributed helpfully to our thinking, which gave us greater confidence in their ability to do the job. Had Firm A produced something half as good, it would have got the job; as it was, Firm B won the contract.

The message therefore is that you should seek opportunities to add value in a proposal. This can be by an insightful appraisal of a client's situation: helping the client to gain a clearer understanding of the circumstances in which you are going to deliver your consultancy services.

Sometimes it may be possible (and helpful) to prepare a proposal in draft and send this for comment to a close contact in the client organization involved in the buying process. It can then be refined to meet the client's needs more closely. (This can be part of a sophisticated selling technique: by getting the client's involvement in producing the proposal, it is seen as a joint problem solving process rather than selling.)

Presenting the proposal

A proposal is at least a written record of what has already been orally agreed with the client. A presentation, however, allows the client to assess the individual consultants. It is a form of sales meeting, albeit structured in a format somewhat different from other meetings. The risk at this point is that you become 'proposal orientated': you regard the presentation as only an oral proposal.

The practical aspects of presenting a proposition will be dealt with in the next chapter. Suffice it to say at this point that it is important to understand why the client is interested in a presentation, and what they hope to get out of it. You can then tailor your presentation against these criteria.

ORGANIZING FOR SELLING

Selling and operating will be done by the same person who is a sole practitioner and (potentially) by different people in a large practice. It is in this latter case that problems of organizing the sales function arise because of the variety of people who might be in contact with a client on just a single project. This problem is compounded when there are several projects in which the firm is engaged with a single client and when there are several buyers of consultancy within the client organization – for example, different business divisions.

Should the firm attempt to coordinate all its engagements with the client through one of its own partners or directors? Alternatively, should it have different account managers to deal with the different parts of the business? Managers of consultancy practices have frequently agonized over the type of organization that is best. I know of one firm that tinkered with its structure twice a year in an attempt to optimize its performance – without success; it is now out of business. There are some general principles that can suggest the structure and processes that should be followed.

All consultants have some responsibility for selling

Everybody in a consultancy practice should recognize the importance of selling, and should be encouraged to take some responsibility for selling. Usually this is limited at the most junior levels to identifying sales opportunities with existing clients, with greater responsibilities for selling increasing with rank and experience.

Not all consultants have the desire or aptitude to sell

It necessarily follows that there has to be some distinction in roles and responsibilities. A practice may distinguish between:

- 'finders' (or 'hunters');
- 'minders' (or 'farmers');
- 'grinders' (the project team).

The targets and expectations of how a consultant allocates his or her time might reflect this. Figure 4.5 below gives an example of this.

In each case we assume that there are 200 days per annum to be allocated (the rest being given over to holidays, training, administration, product development, etc). The 200 days are invested in different ways according to the role of the consultant. A key figure

		New sales	Extension sales	Fee earning
Finder	Days allocated	120	40	40
	Days sold	600	400	40
	Conversion ratio	5	10	1
Minder	Days allocated	40	80	80
	Days sold	120	400	80
	Conversion ratio	3	5	1
Grinder	Days allocated	10	30	160
	Days sold	30	120	160
	Conversion ratio	3	4	1

Figure 4.5   Targets for finders, minders and grinders

to monitor is the conversion ratio – the 'return on investment' for time. The figures shown in Figure 4.5 are illustrative only; each practice needs to work out what is realistic according to its experience, but it is worth noting:

● Finders are expected to be more skilled at selling than the others.

● Time spent in extension selling (selling to existing clients) should yield better results than new sales.

● Time allocated to fee earning is fully used as such. This means that selling will be fitted around fee earning for a grinder.

All consultants engaged on projects should seek out and identify opportunities for further work for the consultancy practice

Opportunities can arise from a variety of sources, most often concerning an aspect of a client's business that is causing dissatisfaction or an area for development. When such a possibility arises, the consultant should probe to find out what the real need is. Other points to consider are: Does the client consider the problem important? Does the client need external resources to resolve the problem?

A project team is well placed to identify extension opportunities; this topic should be on the agenda at each progress review meeting. More generally, skill in identifying high-quality extension opportunities should be an aspect against which the performance of all consultants is assessed. They can help in supporting extension selling by providing intelligence and providing introductions to key members of client staff.

Once an opportunity has been identified, you need to decide in what way it should be best exploited. All extension business must go through the same qualification and conversion procedures as new business. Although a particular consultant may have identified the opportunity, there may be others within the practice who are better able to convert the opportunity into a profitable sale.

You have to be clear on the salesperson's contribution to the selling process

Only if you are clear on what you want the salesperson to contribute can you plan how to run the selling function. If the salesperson is simply a broker between the resources of the consultancy and the needs of clients, what is his or her particular contribution? Is it a knowledge of a business sector or a network of contacts? Is it a capability in seeing the applications of, say, business process re-engineering to organizations, or access to particular skills in the firm? Or a combination of some or all of these?

I have come across all these attributes in various amounts in consultancy salespeople in different practices. Each reorganization emphasizes a different aspect; this year we will be organized in market related teams, whereas last year we belonged to mini-practices based on different functional specializations. The danger of frequent change is that in the new organization the salesperson's assets (networks, leads, sales initiatives, etc) built up over the previous period become devalued, and he or she has to start building afresh.

Another difficulty is that the salesperson does not see his or her role in the same way as the firm's management. It is all very well to claim that the salesperson should be the facilitator of the sale, but salespeople like to be heroes. They need their clear successes; facilitation does not provide this, so human nature will resist some types of organizational role.

Wittreich's (1966) rule number 3 (see Chapter 5) states that, 'A professional service can only be purchased meaningfully from someone who is capable of rendering the service. Selling ability and personality by themselves are meaningless.' This means that it will always be difficult to organize a consultancy sales force along the lines of that for a tangible product.

Much of the work in sales management in a firm therefore consists of resolving the tensions between specialist and selling activities.

Resourcing the bid process

Bidding requires a finite time. For small assignments, the salesperson and/or prospective project manager may prepare the bid; in larger ones, there may need to be more people involved. Because of the pressure to keep up fee earning time, it can be difficult to get consultants to work on a bid in some consulting practices.

But bidding is a project itself, and should be managed as such. The salesperson must make sure that he or she has the right resources to carry it out. This means in particular having consultants with the technical specialisms needed available to work on the bid. Ideally the bid team should form (the core of) the project team that is to undertake the assignment if it is won.

MONITORING SALES PERFORMANCE

Monitoring sales performance is important for two reasons: 1) it shows what the level of future sales is likely to be, and where sales effort needs to be directed; 2) successful sales performance can be analysed to identify what were the reasons for success and hence provide a guide to good practice.

For the purposes of monitoring sales performance a client can be allocated to stages in the selling process as follows:

1. *Sales development.* When sales activities are aimed at developing a relationship with the client, but when there is no specific project in view.

2. *Prospect.* Where there is a specific project (or projects) in view, but for which the practice has not yet received a request for a proposal or invitation to tender from the client.

3. *Proposal.* A proposal has been submitted to the client that the practice should carry out a specific project.

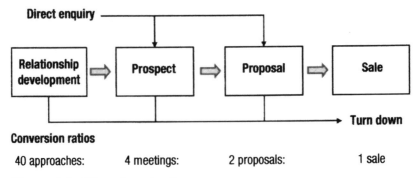

Figure 4.6 The sales pipeline

4. *Sale*. When the client has accepted a proposal and it is now in the order book.

The whole process can be thought of as a leaky pipeline (see Figure 4.6); at each stage, prospective clients will drop out until only a few are left that lead to sales. As well as clients arising from sales development, prospects and proposals may derive from direct enquiries. There will also be clients lost at each stage (called turn downs) because of, for example, the deferral or cancellation of a project, or a contract that is awarded to a competing provider of consultancy services. Figure 4.6 shows the ratios that were calculated by one consultancy salesperson.

Clearly the ratios will vary with time, product, market and salespeople. On the figures shown, on an average of the 40 prospects the salesperson started with, only one resulted in a sale. The significance of this is that if you are to be a successful hunter

Account manager	Client	Current position	Next action	By when

Figure 4.7 Relationship development record

Account manager	Client	Possible project	Likely revenue	Probability	Current position	Next action	By when

Figure 4.8 Prospects record

you have to start with a large number of organizations that you believe could be clients for your service. You have to accept a lot of 'Nos' with only a few 'Yes's'. Sales performance will be measured by the volume of business (number of clients, value of projects, etc) at each stage in the sales process; the conversion of business from one stage to the next.

To this end, sales activity needs to be monitored, and examples of the type of information that can be recorded are shown in Figures 4.7–4.9. These show the information on forms, but it is more normal to keep the data on a computer database. These should be updated regularly. The layout of the records means that the status of the sales process to a client can be quickly assessed, and action taken to follow up where required.

Account manager	Client	Project	Value	Probability	Current position, competition etc	Next action	By when

Figure 4.9 Proposals record

Sales development record

Sales development is the development of a relationship with a potential client, targeted as being a likely buyer of your services. It should be the responsibility of a salesperson assigned to that target. A sales development record is shown in Figure 4.7.

It takes some time to develop clients in this category into prospects, and it is easy to let this category get too small. You should therefore review on a regular basis whether the level of activity in this category is sufficient.

Prospects record

Prospects can arise from either potential clients already identified in the sales development process or direct enquiries. New prospective projects with clients for whom you are currently working should be included here.

The record in Figure 4.8 has spaces for the project for which the salesperson hopes the client will issue an invitation to tender, the likely revenue and an estimate of the probability that a sale will indeed follow. A separate calculation can then be made of the sum of the probable revenues. Actual sales often turn out to be lower, but this figure gives a measure of the probable sales in the pipeline. This can be used as an indicator of possible future peaks and troughs of sales, which would have implications for revenue and resource utilization. Again, you may prefer to use the EDIT process shown in Figure 4.4 to indicate the stage of maturity of any prospective opportunity.

Proposals record

The record in Figure 4.9 is similar to the prospects form, except that only firm proposals are recorded. Here, the sum of the probable sales is a good measure of future workload. Risks to monitor particularly on this record include: a high-value proposal of low probability that will place a high demand on resources if it should sell and a low total probable revenue combined with high probabilities is a sign that future workload might be low if the probabilities have been over-estimated.

Other uses

It is important to monitor the conversion rate from one stage to the next. Key ratios to monitor are: number of sales divided by number of proposals; and value of sales divided by value of proposals. Typically in management consultancy these figures might be one-third to a half – that is, only one in two or three proposals is accepted. If the ratio becomes too low, this can be a sign that either you are bidding for the wrong business, or that your proposals are insufficiently competitive. Likewise, a high conversion rate might indicate opportunities for business expansion. Reasons for proposals being turned down should be monitored through win–lose reviews with the client so that conversion performance can be improved.

Of course, the records need to be kept up to date. This means being honest about those prospects that show no sign of turning into business. It is a matter of judgement which clients should remain on the Sales development and Prospects records. You may wish to remove a prospective client from the sales records if the likelihood of any revenue deriving from the effort is low.

Finally, use these sales records as a basis for improvement. Review performance to find out what techniques are successful, and which clients are the best bets. Distinguish successful performance from unsuccessful, and so build up an understanding of what constitutes good selling practice for your consultancy firm.

DEVELOPING SALES PERFORMANCE

It is always fascinating to get feedback from clients on their perceptions of consultants. I belong to a group of freelance consultants who, from time to time, organize a clients' forum at which selected clients are invited to give feedback on their experience in using consultants. At one of these forums a client, who had invited tenders for a consultancy contract worth £500,000, commented on the mixture of responses he got: 'The worst compensated for their incompetence by their arrogance; they couldn't answer simple questions. The ones we appointed were the opposite – technically excellent. Moreover they were sensitive to the cost implications of the project and ensured we had the financial resources to implement the changes required.' Another client commented, 'The consultant made it easy for us to buy – it was not hard work for us. At no time did we feel that we were being sold to.'

Consultancy firms nowadays often solicit feedback from prospects and clients on their performance, after a sales effort or on the completion of a project. Follow-up after a sales effort should be implemented irrespective of whether the effort resulted in success.

One head of a firm tells an interesting story concerning one of his fellow directors, who asked a prospect what had clinched the sale in favour of his own practice. The client replied, 'It's because your people looked more like a team than the competition.' The director probed to find out what had led the client to this conclusion. 'A very simple thing,' replied the client, 'when your competitors made their presentation two of their team gave a disparaging look concerning the third, who was presenting.' How frightening to think that a major sale was affected by such a simple piece of body language! But what helpful intelligence in managing sales training.

One of my associates talks about organizations that seem to have a 'sales prevention department'. Presumably no organization has the aim of preventing sales, any more than a salesperson would wish to have the negative effect quoted above. Yet everybody who is involved in selling will have experienced occasions when they leave a sales meeting knowing that they have failed. The failure is not that the customer did not want to buy – that possibility always has to exist if you want to be anything more than a high-pressure salesperson. The failure is because the customer might well have bought, but poor selling technique resulted in the salesperson failing to convert the opportunity to a sale.

There are no techniques that will guarantee success in selling consultancy every time. But a good management process, which enables lessons to be learned and applied from experience, will enhance selling performance.

5

Conducting specific sales transactions

BECOMING A CONSULTANCY SALESPERSON

The revenue of a consultancy practice depends on sales but it is a rare business that receives enough orders without any selling effort. So, one of the activities that consultants need to undertake is selling. Career advance in any profession usually involves taking on commercial responsibilities, yet many professionals recoil when contemplating selling. Few will have considered it as a career and fewer still will have previous experience of selling. The addition of consultancy to the product portfolio of other businesses (such as IT companies) in recent years, however, has meant that established sales forces have needed to sell consultancy.

It is said that the skilled salesperson can sell anything, which implies that there is a set of selling skills that are universally applicable. Whether this is true is debatable. Certainly there will be salespeople who find little difficulty in making the transition to selling consultancy from selling more tangible items. But there are several significant differences between these activities, and understanding the implications of these differences will help in selling consultancy. Likewise, the consultant who has no previous selling experience needs some guidance as to the appropriate sales processes to use in selling consultancy. There are challenges for both.

Challenges for the experienced salesperson

Even products that can be customized are usually broadly prede-fined offerings, which may be tailored in detail to the needs of the client. Much of the time, consultancy is the opposite. It starts with identifying the needs of the client (or responding to a set of needs as embodied in an invitation to tender) and then putting together an offering that helps the client to address these needs. This means that – unless you are a consultant with only one product – it is unusual to sell consultancy by going to a client with a preconception of what you are going to sell him or her. Selling is more often about spotting opportunities than creating needs. The implications for you if you are a traditional salesperson are therefore:

- Each consultancy project is a uniquely tailored offering. A car salesperson might sell from a product catalogue; the only variations are the extras that a customer might want. In consultancy, the sales process involves product definition.

- You must listen to clients' requirements and respond with offerings that reflect their needs.

- If you work for a large firm of consultants, you cannot have a comprehensive knowledge across all fields of its consultancy offerings, and so you will need to involve specialists in support selling.

The role of salesperson in consultancy is more one of facilitator than 'hero'. You have to create opportunities that others will help to realize.

Figure 5.1 shows the critical dimensions in thinking about the role of the salesperson. The figure shows two extremes; it is unlikely that any sales activity will be wholly at one end or the other, but will be somewhere in between. What the figure points out, though, is the thrust in selling consultancy; for those whose experience lies in selling products, the challenge lies in moving towards the right in the diagram. The spectrum of selling is shown from being transaction oriented to relationship oriented. A salesperson who is strongly transaction oriented will be impelled to close the sale. In an extreme form this is typical of the high-pressure salesperson, who has a prime objective to ensure that you buy.

Product	Material goods ⟷	Consultancy
Nature of the product	Tangible	Intangible
Orientation	Transaction	Relationship
Who specifies it	Producer	Client
Sales preoccupation	What we want to sell	What the client wants to buy
Basis of evaluation	Quality of the product	Quality of the person

Figure 5.1 The selling spectrum

Salespeople who want repeat business recognize early in their careers that they cannot be wholly transaction oriented. Of course, the quotas and targets that they are set are usually related to sales volume – no points for having wonderful relationships and no sales – but they will be anxious to preserve a good relationship with their customers.

Consultancy, too, has quotas and targets, but the need for a good relationship is even greater than with other products. When buying a tangible item you can see an example of what you will get; in consultancy you buy only a promise. Even if the consultancy has a proven track record, this is no guarantee of success on this occasion; it simply reduces the sense of risk. So there has to be a high level of trust between the salesperson and his or her client. But as with other successful client relationships, once they are firmly established, consultancy clients become a fruitful source of continuing business.

Challenges for the technical specialist

There are challenges for the technical specialist who becomes involved in selling. As for the salesperson, there will be some who make the transition very easily; others find it difficult to accept a sales role. Some specialists feel selling is 'unprofessional', and are most uncomfortable when called on to do it.

Figure 5.2 Factors influencing selling performance

In such circumstances they may rely on their technical expertise, or the warmth of their relationships with the client to secure the sale. But as Figure 5.2 shows, there are three factors that combine to influence the selling performance of a professional:

- *Technical skills.* The specialist skills of the consultant.

- *Interpersonal skills.* In the short term, these are the skills of conducting effective personal relationships. In the longer term, these are manifest as the consultant's network, which needs to be established, maintained and developed.

- *Selling skills.* Understanding buying and selling processes in consultancy, and capability in identifying opportunities and developing sales.

All three are important. The area of the triangle in Figure 5.2 depends on the length of all three sides, so if the length of one side is nil, then the area will be nil. If the area of the triangle represents sales performance, all three skills must be represented to achieve a satisfactory standard of sales performance. What consultants and other professionals often feel reluctant to admit is that selling skills are important. The figure shows, however, that selling skills are as important as the other two.

THE INGREDIENTS OF SELLING PERFORMANCE

Let's now consider each of the factors shown in Figure 5.2.

Technical skills create reputation

Ultimately, the capacity to execute assignments well will be the determinant of a consultancy practice's success. Reputation counts for a lot; in my first week as a consultant I was told, 'One bad job costs 100 good ones.' Satisfied clients act as connectors to fresh business; and satisfied individuals who change jobs introduce their favoured consultants to their new employers. Technical skill creates a favourable reputation, which helps the extrinsic selling process mentioned in Chapter 4.

Interpersonal skills create a network

As noted above, all experienced salespeople recognize the need for their activities to be relationship rather than transaction led if they are to achieve more than a single sale. Research supports common sense that we will buy more from the salesperson we like than one to whom we are indifferent, other factors being equal.

But because of the nature of the consultancy product, far more emphasis has to be placed on the relationship. The reason is that despite references and reputation, when a client buys a consultancy assignment, it is on trust. The project may be expensive and of considerable moment; a buyer may have staked his or her reputation on its success. Before doing this, he or she must have the confidence that it will be successful. It is unlikely that this will be the case unless there is a good relationship with the consultant. This relationship has to be underwritten by good work, however. If the consultant (or consultancy) has previously carried out high-quality work, the client will be more inclined to give them more. This is supported by the evidence that the greater part of consultancy work derives from existing or previous clients.

During your work, you will build up a network of relationships with people who are employed by past or prospective clients, professional contacts and so on. 'Networking' is about maintaining these relationships. This can be done quite easily, by attending business or professional meetings, or even over lunch. I remember sitting at lunch with a partner in a firm of consultants (with whom I was networking!) who complained about his consultant team: 'As we sit here, they are all sat at their desks eating sandwiches. Why aren't they out networking?'

Some 80–90 per cent of a consultancy's sales come from its network – some two-thirds from repeat business and the remainder from referrals. Even if the activity is not directly related to a sale, there are benefits in networking:

- getting market intelligence;

- obtaining leads and introductions;

- raising awareness of your firm and its services;

- maintaining the network.

So consultants have to be active in creating and maintaining their networks. But time spent on networking has to be invested with a purpose; it is easy to be a busy fool, and there are people who are time-wasters, as there are in any other area of activity; beware of them.

Selling skills are needed to create sales

Shortly after I started my first job as a management consultant there was one of those periodic downturns in the market. All consultants are exhorted to sell, and in a recession we were doubly so. Being young and enthusiastic, I started to try to sell to my (limited) network. My sales patter was simple: 'Consultancy is jolly good, and so is my firm. Why don't you buy an assignment?' I was totally unsuccessful, because I had no selling skills. The unhappy truth is that technical skills and a good relationship will create few sales by themselves. Selling skills are also required and the remainder of this chapter deals with this topic.

PURPOSES OF SELLING – WHAT WE ARE TRYING TO ACHIEVE

The simple explanation of 'what we are trying to achieve' is a sale. But as we have seen in Chapter 4, it is rarely a single stage process – there are several steps and these form the basis of a conversion process.

Conversion is the activity of developing clients to successive stages of the sales process. The skills of doing this are in conducting key transactions with the prospective client; these are covered later in this chapter. Suffice to note at this point that it is sensible to monitor your success at conversion at each stage of the sales process, and to research the reasons for success or failure. By monitoring conversion performance you can identify areas of strength and weakness, and develop a better idea of what practices will help you to optimize your conversion rate.

But conversion is not adequate by itself. You also need to qualify: qualification involves choosing which prospective clients to pursue. This is important because it relates to the effective use of time. The consultancy salesperson should be devoting his or her time to pursuing those prospects that are most likely to produce sales.

Qualification

At each stage of the sales process there is a need for qualification: deciding where to invest your time and effort. You need to decide which clients should be converted to the next stage of the sales process, or which sales opportunities with a particular client should be pursued.

Obviously, clients may disqualify themselves: a sales call may be unsuccessful, or a prospect may not agree to a meeting. What is particularly hard for the salesperson, however, is to disqualify a client from the consultancy's point of view. It is hard because the salesperson may well have put much effort in to nursing the prospect to this stage in the sales process.

There are several obvious reasons for disqualification. Some people love to chat to consultants and to pick their brains, with no real intention of offering an assignment. If the assignment in view is one that the consultancy cannot do, or is of questionable ethics, or involves an actual conflict of interest, then the opportunity may also be disqualified. Early in the sales process, therefore, you should assess the probability of a consultancy project deriving from your efforts. To this end, you should check that:

- there is a genuine need for consultancy work of the kind that the consultancy can offer;

- the prospective client intends to offer this to outside consultants;

- the individuals with whom you are dealing have the budget and authority to proceed with the project, or can act as connectors to such individuals.

Qualification is even more crucial at the time of preparing a proposal, not only because the task is time-consuming, but also because the proposal is a commitment by the consultancy to carry out a specified assignment. Before offering to submit a proposal, therefore, you should consider the following:

- Is the consultancy able to carry out the work, in terms of the competence and availability of resources?

- What are the risks involved, and are they acceptable? Risks to be considered include:

  - the financial standing of the client;

  - political risks;

  - the difficulty of achieving the project deliverables;

  - the complexity and size of the project.

- Will undertaking the project produce any *actual* conflicts of interest with respect to any existing clients?

- Will undertaking the project produce any conflicts of interest with other parts of the consultancy?

- Is there a serious chance of winning the assignment?

Salespeople are strongly impelled to make sales and so there is the temptation to bid in response to every invitation to tender. The failure to qualify properly, however, can result in either wasting time, or committing to projects that are unprofitable at best.

Demonstrating the quality of your consultancy in the sales process

Consultancy may appear to a client to be an undifferentiated product; if the client has specified what is to be achieved and the steps towards this, then any capable consultant could probably deliver. Differentiation must therefore lie not only in the consultancy service, but also in the quality of its delivery. Differentiation of delivery starts in the sales process, so what should you be seeking to achieve in this?

Beginners in selling often believe that with their client references, product knowledge and technical skills, a client will be persuaded to buy. Collectively, in the sales jargon, these can be called 'proofs', and they are undoubtedly important. They must, however, be complemented by skill in conducting the sales process; both are vital.

Wittreich, in a seminal article (1966) suggested there were three objectives in selling professional services to be kept in mind:

1. *Minimizing uncertainty:* a professional service must make a direct contribution to the *reduction of the uncertainties* involved in managing a business. The proper assessment of a service, unlike tangible goods, usually must take into account the impact of its performance on the client's business.

2. *Understanding problems:* a professional service must come directly to grips with a fundamental problem of the business purchasing that service. The successful performance of the service, far more so than the successful production of a product, depends on an understanding of the client's business.

3. *Buying the professional:* a professional service can only be purchased meaningfully from someone *who is capable of rendering the service.* Selling ability and personality by themselves are meaningless.

The importance of these concepts has been endorsed by research in the United Kingdom. In 1988, KPMG Peat Marwick McLintock published the findings of some research they had commissioned from MORI. It showed that the relative importance of factors involved in selecting a management consultancy was as shown in Figure 5.3.

Figure 5.3 Selecting a management consultancy – research by MORI for KPMG

One of the two factors ranked as most important is 'having a real understanding of your needs', confirming Wittreich's first two objectives above. Many of the other factors relate to the quality of the people: Wittreich's third objective. In a large consultancy practice, however, the person who is the account manager (maybe a partner or director of the practice) will not necessarily be delivering the service. This is when team selling is used, which is covered later in this chapter.

Although fee levels are shown in Figure 5.3 to be less important comparatively, they can be instrumental in the buying decision in competition when other features of competing firms are very similar and there is a significant difference in the amounts quoted.

The fact that 'previous work with client' comes so low seems to contradict the comments made elsewhere about existing clients being the most fertile ground. The same survey, however, notes that 'Business colleagues were the most important source of information about management consultancies.' Previous work together may not be significant in the intrinsic selling process (that is, to win a particular assignment), but is important in getting you through the door in the first place (that is, being invited to tender) – the extrinsic selling process.

THE SALES PROCESS

Key steps in the selling process

There are three key steps involved in practical selling:

1. Identifying potential clients, getting access to them and establishing a dialogue with them.

2. Conducting sales transactions (telephone calls, meetings), which should lead to an invitation to tender (ITT). An ITT need not be a formal document – it can be an oral request from a prospect for you to put in a proposal.

3. Converting the ITT to a sale.

The framework within which these activities are applied may be ad hoc, or it may be part of a focused, proactive sales campaign to get new clients.

Large consultancies with extensive networks may have no difficulty getting access to a specific target. With greater resources than small practices, they may invest more in selling to a specific target prospect. For example, they may prepare a detailed presentation, free of charge, on an aspect of the client's business where the consultancy believes there to be a good opportunity of working together. Even with good contacts, however, the number of times you can 'cash in' on a relationship is limited. You can exercise a key contact about a couple of times a year, but goodwill on their side will disappear if they see the meetings are of little value. Selling skills are needed in all cases. In what follows I have assumed that you cannot command the attention of the target and so have to follow a more general sales process.

Managing the selling process

Early in the selling process you will need to judge how much work (for example, how many meetings) is required to win an invitation to tender. In some circumstances the opportunity may arise at the first meeting; this will be the case when your consultancy offering is clearly defined and you have carefully pre-qualified the prospect. For example, a recruitment consultant may have established the prospect's need for recruitment services during a preliminary telephone call. At the initial meeting the consultant will have sold the firm's services extrinsically, so that the prospect feels encouraged to invite the consultant to submit a proposal if there is a vacancy to be filled. In other cases a series of meetings may be required, to do one or more of the following:

- clarify the nature of the consulting project;

- meet others of the client staff who might be involved in the buying process;

- introduce others from the consultancy to help in selling or who might be involved in operating the project.

The criteria described in Chapter 3 are useful to remember in the sales process, namely:

- The client has to recognize that a problem or opportunity exists.

- The client has to believe that it merits attention.

- The client must believe that it is possible to resolve the problem or realize the opportunity.

- The client must see the value of outside consultancy help.

- The client must choose your help.

Remember that it is a competitive market. As well as managing your side of the sales process, you need to be convincing the prospect that you are the right consultancy to undertake the project.

ESTABLISHING A DIALOGUE WITH A PROSPECTIVE CLIENT

In establishing a dialogue with a prospective client, there are three steps:

1. Identify the prospect organization to which you wish to sell.

2. Find out which person you should contact.

3. Approach the prospect with the aim of winning a meeting at which you can present your services.

Identifying prospects

If clients are not forming a queue at your door to do business with you (and if they are, why not put up your fees?) then you have to find new clients. Let us assume that you have to find these by hunting. Some criteria for identifying prospects are suggested in Chapter 3. In any case, you should draw up a prospect profile, that is, the key characteristics of an organization likely to buy your services.

You then have to identify the organizations and individuals within them where you have a good chance of being able to sell your services. You might start by referring to a business directory. Often, however, a directory will not give sufficient information about a business for you to qualify them sufficiently, so some further research needs to be done to find out more. Annual reports and advertising material will provide additional useful data. Other sources include newspaper cuttings and other information services that can be accessed via business libraries or computer databases. Indeed, some computer databases allow you to sort companies according to selected criteria (for example, size, location, industry), which greatly reduces the effort required to do this manually. Happily, there is now a lot of information available on the Internet and so much can be achieved through desk research without moving from your office. The next stage is to approach the prospect.

Who to sell to

Whereas organizations may have sophisticated systems for specifying and purchasing hardware, these are rarely matched by the processes for buying consultancy. In selling assignments, you may find yourself in the position of having to guide the prospect through the buying process. The consultancy sales process is directed towards this, involving, as it does, clarifying exactly what the prospect wants. (It is worth noting, however, that as consultancy has become a major item of expense for organizations, the purchasing process has come under greater scrutiny. There is a trend towards 'rules-based purchasing', led by the public sector, which is intended to provide better value for money and fairer treatment of suppliers. Purchasing departments have yet, however, to develop appropriate methods for buying consultancy in a way that allows for the fact that it is not a commodity.)

The old adage in selling is 'sell to the MAN' – the person who has the Money, Authority and Need. In an organization of any size, these may be different individuals or a variety of committees. Miller and Heiman (1989) have identified the following key prospect roles in the buying process:

- the *user*(s) of the service;

- the *technical buyer*, whose approval is needed, acting as a gatekeeper;

- the *economic buyer*, whose authority is needed to release the funds.

It is difficult if not impossible to identify these from outside, and so the fourth role of *coach* is important. The coach is the member of the prospect organization who is committed to your consultancy's offering and who can provide guidance to (and perhaps influence over) those filling the other key roles.

If you have immediate access to a powerful chief executive as your buyer then this distinction of role is less relevant. In other cases you need to recognize the roles, and the buying process that will be engaged. For example, the situation where a client has been commissioned by his or her board to carry out a study of IT requirements for his or her business, needs a quite different selling process from trying to sell a study on IT to a client who is satisfied with his or her present arrangements.

An important objective early in the sales process is therefore to obtain intelligence about the buying process and the roles of the interested parties. This will enable you to focus your selling effort to best effect.

Approaching the prospect

It is an unusual prospect who would engage management consultants without first meeting them – and an unusual firm of consultants who would agree to work with a client under these conditions. So, meetings are an essential part of the selling process. The purpose of the approach is therefore to secure a selling meeting, preferably

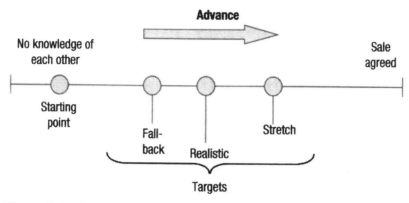

Figure 5.4 Setting targets for a discussion

with the MAN (who, of course, could be a woman!). You may need to do some preliminary research on who might be the MAN, and telephonists and secretaries can be helpful in guiding you to the right person. In situations of any complexity, it may be necessary to identify a coach (see above) as a first step.

CONDUCTING SELLING TRANSACTIONS

Planning a contact discussion – setting targets

You are unlikely to make a significant sale to a new client in the course of a single contact. You will advance to a degree (you hope) with each contact; and by a series of advances achieve a sale. Advance is through a series of discussions – whether by mail, phone or meeting. In planning each contact discussion you need to have an idea of where you are starting from, and to set a realistic target of how far you might get in this discussion. It is also sensible to think about 1) stretch targets – how far you can go if things are going well and 2) fall-back targets – what is the minimum you expect to achieve from the discussion?

Figure 5.4 illustrates the process. At the left-hand side is shown the situation where client and consultancy have no knowledge of each other; at the right hand side is where they have agreed on a sale. The advantage of setting stretch and fall-back targets is that they encourage a more positive frame of mind. With a single target you either make it, or you don't. Under these circumstances it is tempting to set the target low and hence have a better chance of beating it. By contrast, a range of targets enables you to cope with the unexpected during a discussion, without a sense of 'failure'.

There are two main areas in which you need to consider targets. Firstly, *conversion and qualification*. The buying process is the mirror of the sales process. Both aim to establish whether the client and consultancy firm should work together. The conversion and qualification process proceed hand in hand: when the buyer qualifies the consultant to the next stage of the buying process, then the consultant has converted the client to the next stage of the sales process, and vice versa. Secondly, *information gathering*. You need data to:

- specify the nature of the assignment to be undertaken;

- inform the conversion and qualification processes;

- understand the context of the sale – the key players, etc.

The detailed nature of the targets will change as the sale progresses, and they will have a significant influence over what is discussed: the agenda for the contact discussion. But the pursuit of an agenda willy-nilly will have a poor effect on the client relationships.

Although most important at the start of the sales process, relationships remain important throughout. Every contact has an impact on the relationship, and so you need to consider how to ensure that relationships continue to develop favourably throughout and avoid selling activities that may have a negative effect on them, for example, by pressurising the client to buy.

How to approach a prospect

Having identified a prospective client, you have to decide how you will approach them. Should you telephone and ask for an appointment, or do you need to warm him or her up with a letter beforehand? Figure 5.5 illustrates a simple model for developing business with a new client:

Part of the promotional activity of larger consultancies is to circulate their own publicity literature, such as newsletters or business journals to prospective clients. This means that there will already be

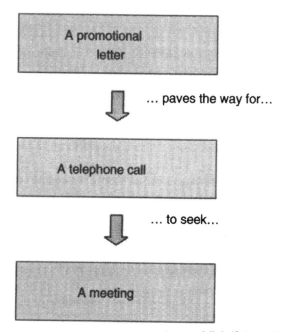

Figure 5.5   Developing business with a new client

some awareness among prospects about the firm and its services. If this is the case, then there may be no need to warm up with a letter beforehand. Even so, promotional material might provide a convenient reason for writing to a client in the first place. For example, you may have recently published a newsletter highlighting a particular project you have carried out. Your letter might suggest (with good reasons!) why such a project might be of interest to the recipient.

Consultants' publicity material may have some sort of response mechanism built in (for example, a tear-off slip that can be returned to register interest or at least an e-mail address to send queries). This means that if approaches are focused on those who have shown interest, a better conversion ratio should result. Nowadays, you might consider an approach via e-mail. Unfortunately, there is so much junk e-mail that unless the recipient knows you there is a good chance that no attention will be paid to your message.

The objective in warming up the prospect is to provide enough information to convince him or her of the benefits of investing time in a telephone conversation, and become inclined towards the idea of meeting you. You are seeking, in fact, to satisfy the qualification process on the prospect's side. If your service can be explained and understood in a simple telephone conversation, this might be the best method of qualification. If it is complicated, or you feel uncomfortable at a direct approach, then writing a letter might be best. You must also consider what you are offering at the first meeting – what are the benefits to the prospect in meeting you. Some executives may be prepared to make time to see consultants speculatively, but rarely simply to hear them give a catalogue of their services. They need to know how the consultancy's services are going to develop business performance and competitiveness, or remedy problems. Sometimes consultants may offer an appraisal of (some aspect of) the business early in the relationship as an incentive. For example, a strategy consultancy might make a presentation on a business's position within its sector, hoping to display a knowledge and capability that will persuade the prospect to do business with them.

If the presentation is to be effective, then the consultancy has to invest time in preparing it. Time should not be invested lightly; the selling team should feel that it is spreading its seed on fertile ground. The presentation is therefore unlikely to be made at the first meeting between consultancy and prospect.

The telephone call

Although telephone technique is a basic selling skill, it is one in which I have found experienced consultants often to be weak. The following notes are therefore intended to summarize the key points.

One of the first challenges is getting through to speak to executives at a prospect. If they are warmed up and expecting you to call, then there is less difficulty. Even so it can be difficult to find a time when the executive is free to speak to you. As a salesperson you will want to keep the initiative and therefore will want to make the call yourself. If there is little incentive for a prospect to call back, it is unlikely he or she will do so. You have to make the call at times when you are free, so you need to know when the executive is likely to be free to receive it. It is best to avoid the core times for meetings: 10.00 am–12.00 pm and 2.00 pm–4.00 pm. Some consultants try to phone before 9.00 am or after 6.00 pm because they might also avoid a protective secretary at those times. Even so, my rule of thumb is that it often takes several telephone calls before you can get to speak to a prospect.

A further hint is to telephone after the hour or half-hour rather than before (that is, at 10.35 rather than 10.25). Meetings usually start on the hour or half-hour, so even if you get through at 10.25 am, the prospect may be about to go off to a meeting, and so have little time to speak. This is less likely to be the case at 10.35 am.

Secretaries (although an increasingly rare breed) are more often helpful than obstructive; ideally, you should make the prospect's secretary your ally in the selling process. Occasionally one might be too protective, asking your business and judging that it is unlikely to be of interest to the boss. If it really is impossible to get past the secretary, or enlist his or her help, you can try the following:

- *Abandon this prospect.* Invest your time in others that might offer a better chance of a sale. After all, an executive's secretary should be able to tell the difference between interesting and unwanted approaches.

- *Try to bypass the secretary.* You need to be convinced of the error of his or her judgement. Moreover, it could be embarrassing to end up talking to the secretary again despite trying to bypass him or her.

- *Find a different point of access.* This could be via another executive in the same organization, seeking an introduction through a mutual acquaintance, or aiming to 'bump into' the executive or an appropriate connector at some business or social function.

A secretary can be helpful in easing communication if the executive is proving inaccessible. A comment from the consultant might be: 'I wrote to Mr Smith last week concerning our services, which we thought might be of particular value to your business at this time. In my letter I said I'd phone to see whether we might meet, and to fix a mutually convenient time.' In my experience, the secretary's response might be: 'Yes, he's asked me to fix a meeting when you rang.' (Great!); 'He asked me to tell you that he's not interested.'; or 'He's not spoken to me about it.' In the last case you might then ask the secretary to find out what the boss wants to do, so that if he or she is not available next time you ring, at least you can stop wasting time if they are not interested. But this is very much a fall-back position if you can't get hold of the boss in the first place.

Nowadays, of course, there is a good chance that you don't actually talk to a human being, but engage with voice mail. Again, you should maintain the initiative – leave a message explaining why you are calling and say when you might call again. If you fail to make contact again, then suggest that the client calls you if they are interested. If they don't call, it means they are not interested and you can avoid wasting more time.

Preparing for the telephone call

Before placing the call, you have to have prepared the structure of the telephone conversation. Preparing what you are going to say is only half the telephone conversation. What are you aiming to find out, as well as to convey, in this conversation? You will want to confirm your understanding of the prospect's needs, the position of your contact in the buying process, and the next steps, at the very least. This is to enable you to qualify the prospect for the next stage.

You will also want to set some objectives for the discussion. There is a series of possible outcomes from a telephone approach:

1. receive an invitation to tender;

2. fix a meeting with the prospect;

3. meeting to be arranged at some future date;

4. send material then contact again;

5. call back at a specified time in future;

6. no interest.

It is unlikely that you get an invitation to tender because the prospect has an immediate need for your services. Even if you did, you would want to qualify this – you are unlikely to put in a proposal without first meeting the prospect.

Next best is that the prospect agrees to a meeting; you have achieved your objective in the telephone approach. The remaining outcomes are of decreasing commercial attractiveness. The reason for showing them, however, is that the outcome is not limited to a simple 'Yes/No' to a meeting. Even if there is no interest in your services now, you may have created a link that brings a prospective client into your network – a link you could probably nurture and exercise profitably at sometime in the future.

Conducting sales meetings

Having got access to your target prospect, the next step is to try to persuade the prospect to invite you to tender for a piece of consultancy work. This is accomplished by conducting one or a series of sales meetings.

Of these meetings, the most important is the initial contact made with each person involved in the buying process: 'You never get a second chance to make a first impression.' Better selling performance derives from stacking the odds more in your favour. The better the first impression, the better the chance of winning the sale. The first meeting, therefore, will have a profound effect on what follows, which is why this is the one on which we will concentrate. Obviously all the others will have some impact, but they will only modify that created at the first. Moreover, the first meeting will be significant as it will be largely instrumental in defining the general areas in which client and consultancy are to work together.

The relationship dimension is crucial. For example, the salesperson who catechizes a senior executive to identify the focus of a project may damage the relationship. Any meeting with a client will affect the relationship with the consultant, and so meetings must have a relationship objective as well as that of content. As indicated in Chapter 3, it may be better not to make a sale but win a worthwhile relationship, rather than the opposite.

Preparation for a sales meeting

Most consultants will nod vigorously when asked, 'Should you prepare for a sales meeting?' but will disagree on what form that preparation should take. If Wittreich's third criterion is to be satisfied (see above), the consultancy salesperson has to be more than simply a broker of useful resources; you have to show the value of the connection between the needs of the prospect's business and the services of the consultancy – for example, how your services will help the prospect address current key business issues. But again, as in the telephone conversation, you must avoid a preoccupation with what you are going to say. There is more extensive comment on the agenda for the first meeting below; for now, you should consider what you need to find out from the prospect, as well as what to say. The quality of questions and comments can serve to impress the prospect (or quite the opposite!).

Consequently you need to consider whether you need to take something along to the first meeting. One of my associates recommends that at the very least you take a printed sheet with a list of points for discussion – not necessarily as formal as an agenda – to the first meeting. The aim is to show that you have given some thought to this particular meeting; it is not a clone of a score of similar meetings you have conducted over the previous months.

Personal impact

The salesperson in consultancy is initially the embodiment of the product. In selling a tangible item, it can be described and displayed. Not so in consultancy: the prospect will endow the consultancy service with the characteristics of the salesperson. Inevitably, the initial meeting will provide the client with a sample experience of working with you.

Consultants learn early in their careers how to dress properly, how to relate to clients and how to manage their body language. These requirements are as relevant to selling as they are to consultancy. It is important to recognize that people take in information through what they see, hear and feel, and use all three channels. People have preferences, so each salesperson will have his or her own preference. The danger is that you will then use that channel exclusively; this will be all right with clients who have the same preference, but less effective with those whose preference is different. So, you need to consider visual aids, the words you use, and the rapport you generate with the prospect.

Opening the sales meeting

For those new to selling, there is a problem about what to say after the initial pleasantries. Figure 5.6 suggests an outline agenda for an initial meeting.

As with meeting anybody for the first time, a meeting will open with pleasantries, to start building a personal relationship. Get the

1. Pleasantries
2. Bridge to the business discussion
3. Probing for prospects' concerns
4. Discussing how these concerns might be jointly addressed
5. Decide next steps

Figure 5.6   Outline agenda for an initial meeting

prospect talking early on; because you have an agenda doesn't mean you have to do all the talking!

There then needs to be a natural bridge to talking about business. This needs to be done by body language as well as orally. Opening your briefcase and bringing out your pad and pen will serve to show that the business of the meeting is going to start.

Some years ago, I had reached this point in my first meeting with a finance director of a prospective client, to whom I had been introduced by the personnel manager, who reported to him. I had some previous discussions with the personnel manager who, I assumed, had briefed the FD. We then commenced the meeting and I proceeded on from the discussions I had with the personnel manager. After about 15 minutes, the FD stopped and said, 'Hang on a minute; what are we talking about here? I'm lost.' The personnel manager had not briefed him, and that was the last meeting I had with that prospect. With that experience behind me, I favour a recap on the background to the meeting as an introduction to the business discussion. This serves to make sure that both you and the prospect are starting from the same point.

A technique that salespeople are sometimes taught is to take 'control' of a meeting. What this means in practice is controlling the agenda. Personally as a prospect, I'm not sure I want to be controlled. The prospect will be coming to the sales meeting with an agenda, even if it is not articulated. The good salesperson will allow for the fact that the prospect has an agenda and will let him or her express it. So, you will perhaps wish to agree on what you are going to cover. If it is a first meeting, it is helpful for you and your prospect each to give a brief summary of your business and where you fit into it.

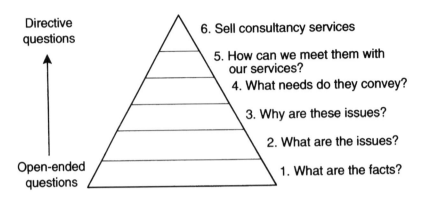

Figure 5.7 The probing pyramid

These first items on the agenda are relatively uncontentious and will serve to help build rapport. Next you have to start to probe for the prospect's concerns and show how your services relate to them. (The probing pyramid technique, set out below, can be used for structuring this part of the meeting.) Finally, as shown in Figure 5.6, you have to agree on the next steps to be taken by both sides following the meeting, which ideally should take the selling process on to the next stage.

The probing pyramid: how to establish the prospect's needs

It can be difficult, however, to decide what questions to ask. What do you need to know? What kind of questioning should you use? I am indebted to my colleague, Dennis Sobey, for introducing me to the concept of the 'probing pyramid', which helps to identify the prospect's needs. Although a simple model, it can provide the basis for an extensive discussion. Once the probing pyramid is understood and put into action, it provides you with both the types of question to ask and the order in which they might be asked, as the meeting – or a series of meetings – progresses. It is particularly useful in planning the first meeting with a new prospect.

The framework is shown in Figure 5.7. The sequence of the agenda is shown on the right. At the start you may discuss facts about the business, but then you need to move on to the issues affecting the business. There are two potential traps at this stage.

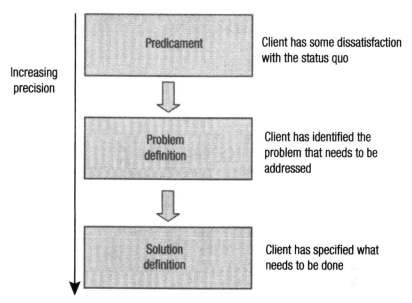

Increasing precision

Predicament — Client has some dissatisfaction with the status quo

Problem definition — Client has identified the problem that needs to be addressed

Solution definition — Client has specified what needs to be done

Figure 5.8　Progressive precision of specification

Firstly, it is tempting, having identified one issue, then to proceed with the next stages. At an initial meeting, if you are to identify other relevant issues, note each issue, and then remain at item 2 in the agenda until you have exhausted this topic, or make sure that you return to it. Secondly, it is tempting to leap straight from item 2 to item 5 without going through items 3 and 4. Items 3 and 4 enable you to focus your response in item 5 in a way that will be attractive to the prospect.

CONVERTING THE ITT TO A SALE

An invitation to tender (ITT) can arise early or late in a sales process and have tight or loose specifications. Figure 5.8 illustrates progressive tightness of specifications.

An example of the invitations to tender at each stage for a consultancy practice could be:

- *Predicament*. How can we sell more to our clients?

- *Problem definition*. How can we develop the performance of our account managers?

- *Solution definition.* Can you deliver a training course for account managers?

A client might be at any of these stages when opening a discussion with a consultant; and the degree of definition may progress during the sales process. Indeed, there is some truth in the saying that 'Selling is free consultancy', but beware of providing excessive value free of charge in order to win a sale. For example, coming up with a robust definition of what 'the underlying problem is' following the client's predicament definition may involve both considerable insight and effort.

An explanation of how to conduct this process is given in Chapter 6 on problem solving; suffice to say that there comes a point when you and the client have agreed that you should submit a proposal. In the sales process (see Chapter 4) this is divided into two parts: 1) *proposition design*, which is about the content of your response and 2) *pitching*, which is how you put it across to the client. The former is dealt with in more detail in Chapter 8 on terms of reference; the latter is dealt with in more detail below. But first, a word of warning: consultants invest a lot of time and effort in preparing proposals, but often the client will have already a predilection to buy – or not – depending on the consultant's performance in the earlier stages of the sales process. So, make sure that you put in sufficient effort early in the sales process.

Submitting a proposal

The proposal is often the only significant written communication in the sales process. Terms of reference set the content and terms of business set the commercial context for a consultancy project. These are usually brought together in the proposal, prepared by the consultancy.

As well as being a contractual document, a proposal has a selling purpose. It must:

- persuade the client to undertake the project (or to endorse a decision already made);
- make the case for engaging consultants;
- set out how the consultancy would approach the assignment;

1. An appraisal of the nature of the client's business, the background of the proposed assignment and the problems to be tackled
2. Definition of the terms of reference and scope of the assignment with comments on the validity and any critical aspects of the terms of reference supplied by the client
3. Proposed approach to the project describing the tasks to be accomplished and the methodology and techniques to be used
4. A work plan indicating the timetable, sequence and duration of tasks and the total elapsed time needed to complete the assignment
5. A statement of the expected results and outputs from the assignment
6. Details of the form and frequency of reporting and arrangements for regular liaison with client staff
7. Proposed staffing levels and roles to be assigned to consulting staff and client counterpart staff and an estimate of the total time inputs proposed
8. Fee and expenses quotation and invoicing procedures (which may be presented separately)
9. Supporting information on the consultancy's services, and relevant assignment experience and curricula vitae of the assignment team members
10. Details of the consultancy's standard terms and conditions (or the terms and conditions applicable to the particular assignment)
11. Methods for assuring the quality of the assignment

Figure 5.9   Contents of a proposal (source: Institute of Management Consultancy)

- convince the client that the consultancy is well equipped to carry out the assignment, and that it should be chosen so to do;

- lay out the terms on which the assignment is to be conducted.

The length, form and complexity of proposal documents will vary widely according to what is appropriate but, in varying degrees of detail, proposals will normally contain the items shown in Figure 5.9. In addition, there will probably be a statement of the benefits of proceeding. If the proposal is long, or complex, it may be helpful to the reader to put in a summary at the beginning to provide a bird's-eye view of the contents.

A proposal is a selling document, which should persuade the client to use your services in carrying out the project. Supporting evidence (covered in item 9 in Figure 5.9) should be tailored to the assignment under consideration. The consultancy therefore must be able to access its assignment experience, particularly if the client wants to take up references. Whether dealing with assignment experience or that of the prospective members of the project team, it should be relevant to the assignment that is under consideration. Standard CVs for consultants are all right as source documents, but they should be tailored for each proposal to highlight the reason an individual consultant is particularly fitted for inclusion on an assignment team.

A proposal should be a manifestation of the value that your consultancy practice can bring to the client. Clients are rarely impressed by statements of how wonderful the consultancy practice is.

Nowadays, organizations are rarely embarrassed by using consultants. Presentations made jointly by consultants and client staff at conferences are not unusual. Nonetheless, references to other clients should be made circumspectly when talking to prospective clients. Bear in mind that prospects will assume that you will discuss them and their business in the same way with your other clients. A client's permission should be sought before discussing with other clients the work you have done for them. From a prospect's view, however, it can be tremendously helpful to talk to an existing client – and a valuable selling aid to a consultancy if given a glowing reference.

The reasons for using your firm should be included in almost every proposal. If the need for the assignment for which you are proposing is already widely accepted, then you may need to do no more. If, however, the sponsor or some of the sponsor's colleagues have yet to be convinced of the benefit of proceeding, then you should make clear the rationale underlying the project and the benefits of proceeding.

Nursing the sale

Once the proposal has been submitted, the sale will need to be nursed. It is rarely satisfactory to submit a proposal and then wait for a 'Yes/No' answer. Ideally the salesperson should know the steps involved in the client's decision-making process and be on hand to deal with any difficulties and to direct attention to the benefits of your undertaking the assignment.

Immediately after submitting the proposal, the salesperson might contact the prospect to:

- check that the proposal has been received;

- get initial reactions and confirm the decision-making process;

- identify any real difficulties the client has in choosing your proposal and deal with intrinsic objections.

On this last point, note that in the private sector particularly, price is only one of several factors that influence a client's buying decision. Classic negotiation on the cost, payment terms and so on may be required, but these are less important than the prospect:

- believing that you have clearly understood his or her company's needs;

- having confidence in the consultancy's people;

- believing that the proposed approach will achieve the benefits claimed.

If a client is unhappy with a proposal, therefore, see this as a joint problem solving process. The client needs consultancy, you want to provide it, so how can this be done to the best advantage of all concerned? When a client expresses concern, the salesperson must probe to find out what that concern really is.

For example, suppose your estimate of the consultancy fees for a particular job is £20,000, and the client is resistant to this. Let's assume that your fee estimate is based on a costing of fee days times fee rate. An obvious option is to attempt to reduce the fees. If, however, your fee rate is realistic and your estimate of the time required is accurate, then reducing the total fee means changing one of these.

The general practice within consultancy firms is to set fee rates annually (or more frequently during periods of high inflation) at a fixed rate for costing purposes. In this environment, this means that a reduction in total fees will show up as a 'loss', that is, the same number of days at a lower fee rate than standard. The result is that there is then some pressure to do the job more quickly, or to use less expensive resources, both of which are likely to diminish quality.

So, go back to the original problem: why is the client wanting to reduce the fees? Is it because they do not think it represents value for money? Or is it because they do not have the budget? If their reservations are about value for money, do you as their consultant truly believe that the benefits of this project adequately outweigh the costs, both actual and opportunity costs? If you do, then the problem is one of communication. The client:

- does not recognize the benefits; or
- does not value the benefits in the same way as you; or
- lacks the confidence that the benefits will accrue.

In these circumstances there is a major job to be done to diagnose which of these applies and then take remedial action. Of course, if the benefits are not worthwhile, should you be advising them to proceed with the project in the first place?

If the client's problem concerns their budget, can the budget be changed? If the answer is no, the onus is upon you to see what you can do to restructure the project within the time allowed by a reduced budget, usually by reducing the scope. I find an effective strategy is to go through this with the client. We go through the tasks and the estimate of times required for each, to see what can be pared. This allows the client to make suggestions that may not have occurred to me, as well as making clear what the effect of the reduced budget will be. Treating this as a serious problem, and engaging in joint problem solving with the client, will also help to build a good relationship between you.

Losing the sale

Not every bid will succeed, but don't lose heart! If you have been sufficiently impressive, you should be invited to be on the tender list for the next piece of consultancy that you could do for that client. Anyhow, a good bid should cement the client relationship, and provide the basis for further discussion about what you have to offer in other areas of consultancy.

DEVELOPING SELLING SKILLS

In this section we consider some of the basic skills that are needed in conducting activities in the selling process.

Basic skills in selling

The danger of being dogmatic over any aspect of selling is that there is almost certainly a salesperson somewhere who, despite breaking any rule you care to mention, is being enormously successful. In many ways, the choice of method of approach is a personal one. Just as the same style of dress would not suit everybody, so too do different salespeople have different styles.

The initial contact with a prospect is crucial in that it forms the background to the sales activity that follows. Making the initial contact is perhaps one of the most stressful parts of the sales activity for the salesperson. The following tips, therefore, although generally applicable in selling consultancy, should be particularly helpful when approaching a prospect for the first time:

- Listen. We have noted that in consultancy the emphasis is on the prospect specifying what they want and why they want it. You can respond only if you first listen to what they have to say.

- Have a positive vision of your transactions with your prospects. If you expect a successful outcome, you are more likely to achieve it than if you expect to fail. Failure is likely to result if you are about to make a phone call to a prospect and have an internal video running that says 'They won't put me through. Even if they do, I'll say all the wrong things. Mr Prospect will ask me all sorts of questions I won't know the answer to...' Contrast this with a view that says 'I expect to be put through. This will give me the opportunity to have a mutually beneficial discussion with Mr Prospect.' You should therefore aim to begin with a positive rather than negative expectation of the encounter. If it helps, write out the positive scenario on a card. Before making a telephone call or entering a meeting read it to yourself. Gradually the positive attitude should begin to take over.

- In particular, you should have a positive vision of your relationship with the prospect. If you see yourself as a supplicant seeking the boon of his or her custom, this will show, and the prospect will treat you as an inferior. The picture you should have in your mind is as fellow professionals with a shared interest – the improvement of the prospect's business. Of course, you will wish to maintain a professional relationship with your clients on matters to do with work, but this does not imply superiority or inferiority; the client is an expert in his or her area of work, as you are in yours.

There are clients who want their egos massaged (don't we all to some extent?). If you don't like doing this then, in cases where it is necessary, you must relinquish the client to someone who is good at ego massage!

Telephone skills

The challenge of making a telephone call is that you have no channel from which to get visual data on how the other person is responding. If the call is to someone that you don't know, it is therefore more difficult to strike up a conversation with him or her than if you meet face to face. My observations from training consultants in this basic skill are:

- When starting the call, smile and perhaps stand. These add energy and friendliness to your voice.

- Slow down at the start of the call. People need to 'tune in' to your voice and will miss information while they are doing so. If you are making a number of calls on the same topic, it is sometimes useful to have a script. Make sure that you use it only as a guide to what you want to say rather than reading it out – it is difficult to sound authentic when reading a script!

- Take your style from that of the person at the other end of the line. If they are brisk and businesslike, so should you be; if they are relaxed and friendly, you should match their style.

The telephone call is a meeting but not one that is face to face and you need to treat it accordingly.

Face to face skills

- You will be better able to deal with a meeting effectively if you are calm. I remember attending an initial meeting with an experienced colleague some years ago. We had to climb to the second floor of the office block and I noticed that my colleague was climbing even more slowly than his senior years required. The reason, he explained, was that he should not reach the client's office out of breath.

- You will be more stressed at the start of a meeting if you are late and you will also create an unfavourable initial impression. The rule is always to arrive in good time with a margin allowed for delays.

- Listen, and show by your body language that you are doing so. Nod encouragingly, ask questions and take notes. Encourage the other person to talk. There will be clients who are verbose or who stray into irrelevancies; bring them back to the topic with a question. You can interrupt without giving offence by saying, 'I wonder if I might interrupt you at this point to ask... ?'

- Use non-evaluative or descriptive statements in your questioning, rather than judgmental ones. For example, don't ask, 'Why has your division failed to meet its profit targets?' Better to ask, 'What are the difficulties that have prevented your division meeting its profit targets?' People will more happily admit to difficulties than failure. The trick is to talk of half-full bottles rather than half-empty ones. (Of course, there are occasions when you will wish to confront a client by using judgmental statements, but this should be by design rather than accident.)

- When questioning, vary the pace. One question rapidly following the last begins to sound like an interrogation. A pause will also serve to show that you are listening.

- Avoid asking double questions; this can be confusing and, most probably you will get answers only to one of the questions. (A double question is of the sort, 'Have things been so difficult in previous years? Do you see an upturn for next year?')

- Another trap is turning open-ended questions into multiple-choice close-ended ones. For example, 'How do you see the future prospects for your business? Will competition increase? Or will there be a general recovery in the sector?' The open-ended question has been lost, and the consultant is leading the client.

Framing questions

Questioning must, of course, not be an interrogation! Happily, however, most people like to talk about their business if asked properly. As the questioning progresses, you gradually move from the use of non-directive, open-ended questions to directive questions. You may also find that the focus of the questioning changes – for example, from dealing with one small part of the organization to issues affecting the organization as a whole.

Use open-ended questions to broaden the discussion. These are the questions that typically begin with Who, What, Why, When, How, Where? Directive questions are the questions prefaced Would, Could, Should, Will, Is, If, May, Can? They restrict the response to a Yes/No answer. They help to check your understanding of the information that has been elicited by the open-ended questions.

In both cases, the pressure of silence may encourage the prospect to open up. What is equally true is that if you are talking, the prospect is not. You need to encourage the prospect by your questioning to give you the information you require.

Of course, people will give information in response not only to questions. An assertion or a comment may also elicit a response. Listen to any popular radio or TV news programme to hear examples of these frequently used.

Team selling

In order to satisfy Wittreich's third criterion, it may be sensible for more than one consultant to attend the sales meeting. Whenever there is more than one consultant attending a meeting with a client, whether it is the first or a subsequent meeting, it is important that you have worked out your respective roles. You should have decided how you are to position yourselves with the client. If the aim is that one of you is to be the leader of the project, if it is sold, then that person must be allowed to establish their credentials with the client.

At the very least, you should decide which of you is to lead the discussion at the meeting. The person who leads should make openings for the other to make a contribution; it doesn't help the selling process to be fighting over airtime. It is also incumbent on the person in the secondary role to respond to the openings provided by the leader. Some years ago, I was in a sales role and took along a technical expert to meet a prospect. I kept on making opportunities for him to contribute, passing the conversation over to him with comments like 'Wouldn't you say that was the case?', but he refused to respond. It was like serving tennis balls to someone who made not the slightest effort to return them. Eventually, the prospect got tired of this and asked me, 'Who's this then – your pet parrot?' That was the last meeting with that prospect.

Dealing with objections

Objections come in two forms: 1) extrinsic, which are general, to do with using consultants, your firm or you; and 2) intrinsic, which are about the specific details of your proposition.

Extrinsic objections tend to come earlier on in the sales process; if you cannot deal with them satisfactorily then, you will find it difficult to progress. In dealing with them make sure that the objection is not based on a false assumption or misapprehension and probe to find out what the real concern is. Be prepared to handle the most common objections; remember that it is not only the answer itself, but the manner in which it is given that will inspire confidence. So, make a checklist of the extrinsic objections that have given the most difficulty, and prepare suitable answers to handle them.

Intrinsic objections give you information about the client's needs that will enable you to refine your proposition. Again, it is worth probing to find out what the real concern is. You need also to make sure you elicit all objections before revising your proposition, and here the 'trial close' is useful. The trial close is an 'if... then...' statement: 'If we bring the price down to meet your budget, then would you proceed?' is an example. It avoids wasting time only partially satisfying a client's needs when there are other objections to be dealt with.

Developing selling skills

Whether you win or lose a sale, you should carefully analyse the result and apply the lessons to future sales efforts (the process

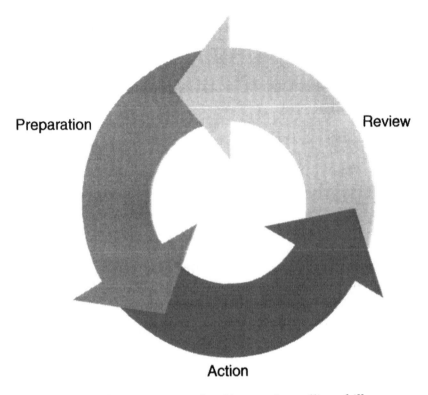

Figure 5.10 The virtuous circle of improving selling skills

shown in Figure 5.10). They may be surprising. For example, some years ago one consultancy won a job and asked, 'Why us?' It emerged that a reason for its success was that it used colour slides in its presentation! The client interpreted the investment in (what was then) more expensive colour as a significant commitment to the project.

Getting better at selling may mean doing different things or doing things differently. The virtuous circle of improvement shown in Figure 5.10 is helpful in thinking about how to do this.

Although the focus in selling is on action, it has to be preceded by careful preparation. After action, you review how things have gone, so that your preparation will be better informed next time. All three steps need to be carried out carefully to improve performance.

At the end of a sales activity, which has culminated in putting a proposal to a client, conduct a win–lose review with the client.

Find out from them why they selected you, or why you failed to get the contract. Throughout the selling process make it clear that this is something that you intend to do – and experienced purchasers of consultancy will expect to do it anyhow. It will yield invaluable information that will help you to develop your selling performance.

6

Consultancy problem solving

THE VARIED NATURE OF PROBLEMS

In Windsor Great Park there is a path, or more accurately an avenue, called the Long Walk. Extending for three miles in a straight line, it passes through the park towards Windsor Castle. The path is wide – you can wander within its limits, but its boundaries are clear – and, as you walk along it, the prospect of the Castle is always in view. Some consultancy projects are like that path and are conducted by using a standardized approach. From start to finish the path – the series of tasks required to conduct the project – is clear. There may be minor deviations along the way but these will be within the broad boundaries. The outcome will be as clearly in sight as Windsor Castle.

By contrast, there are other consultancy projects that are forays into unknown territory. Like the search for El Dorado, these projects seek a goal that is believed to exist but its detailed nature, its location and the path there are uncertain. Such projects are needed when unprecedented or peculiar problems (often called 'messy' or 'wicked') have to be addressed. As with a journey into the unknown, it is easy on these projects to lose your way; to take wrong turnings; to waste time; to fail to meet the goal. But first you must recognize that you have to deal with a messy problem. The consultant unaware of this is like the young army officer, whose colonel wrote of him, 'Undoubtedly there are soldiers who would follow this officer but, if so, it would be only out of a sense of curiosity to find out where he was going.'

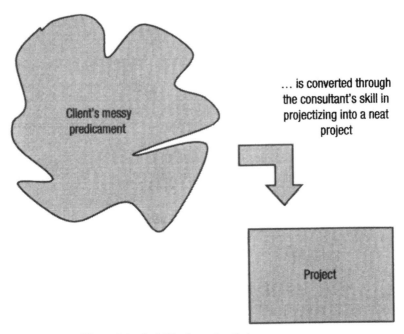

Figure 6.1   The critical skill of projectizing

There is a poem about six blind men encountering an elephant for the first time. Each feels a different part of the elephant – hide, tusks, trunk, legs etc – and confidently asserts (quite wrongly), the properties of an elephant based on his limited information. Organizations are like the elephant and those of us who engage with them are like the blind men; at best we have a partial view. If you take a systems view of an organization, then everything is connected to everything else. You therefore have to define some boundaries to the area of your study, otherwise you will be faced with an impossibly complex task in addressing an organizational issue.

The challenge for the consultant is where to draw the boundaries; focus on the wrong area and your intervention may be ineffective. This challenge is depicted in Figure 6.1: clients are faced with many predicaments but well-defined, time and resource bounded projects are designed by consultants to address them. Of course, there will rarely be a perfect fit between predicament and project, but the quality of fit will be a function of how well the consultant understands the client's situation and designs an appropriate approach. It is this skill that this chapter addresses.

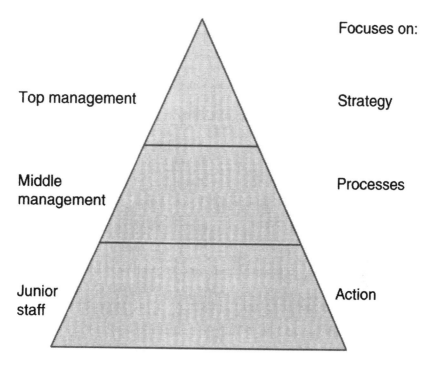

Figure 6.2 A simple model of business organization

The structure of business problems

A simple model of a business organization is illustrated in Figure 6.2.

Top management is preoccupied with the direction of an organization – its strategy; middle management is preoccupied with the design of the infrastructure that enables the strategy to be achieved – process design and operation. Junior staff take action within this framework. Consultants may assist at all levels, but all three are interdependent. In particular, processes can be defined only in the context of a strategy, whilst activity has to be within the process framework – the level above creates boundaries, except in the case of strategy. (Incidentally, I am giving a broad definition here of strategy.)

The consultants who engage at these three levels can be designated strategic, functional and technical, and the characteristics of the problem in which they engage are shown in Figure 6.3.

Organizational concern	Type of consultant	Type of problem
Strategy	Strategic	Many degrees of freedom; problems ill defined; solutions unbounded
Process Action	Functional Technical	Few degrees of freedom; problems well defined; solutions bounded

Figure 6.3 Consultants and problems

The variety of consultancy problems

Technical consultancy is not confined to technology, but also includes consultancy that is carried out by specialists applying standard techniques, for example:

- a recruitment consultant, finding a suitable candidate to fill a job vacancy;

- an accountant advising on a company's tax affairs;

- an IT consultant, advising on the choice of computer system.

On the whole, questions are easier to identify and the answers easier to define at the technical level. For example, a recruitment consultant may be retained to find a candidate for the position of Marketing Director for a client. The question is clear; so too are the features of the answer – the consultant needs to provide the client with a shortlist of suitable, qualified candidates.

Problem solving consists of the process to be followed leading to the answer. In the case of recruitment, the process is likely to follow the sequence shown below:

1. Get job description for new position.

2. Identify key aspects of business and environment in which the new appointee will be working.

3. Determine contents of remuneration package and scope for negotiation.

4. Agree person specification with client.

5. Agree an advertising campaign and copy to be used.

6. Place adverts.

7. Sort responses. Identify long list for interview.

8. Interview and identify suitable candidates.

9. Provide client with shortlist of names and reports on each.

This is a clear process, akin to the Long Walk described at the start of this chapter. By contrast, the questions and answers responding to a client predicament around, say, 'How should we engage best with Western Pacific economies?' are much more like the hunt for El Dorado. But equally, a process is needed to engage with these types of problems.

Of course, technical consultants will seek to reassure themselves of the soundness of the assumptions underpinning their project. Thus, in the examples above:

- A recruitment consultant will want to understand the current operations of a business and how it is likely to develop, before advising on the recruitment of a senior executive.

- An accountant will need to understand the corporate structure and how it might change before advising on optimizing tax.

- An IT consultant will need to know how the requirements of a business are likely to develop before advising on the choice of computer.

If a client cannot provide satisfactory answers to these questions, then there may be functional or strategic consultancy work that needs to be done before a project in a technical area can proceed. Sometimes consultants are accused of commercial opportunism, setting out to enlarge the scope of their projects beyond those set by clients, when in fact extra work is required to provide a sufficiently sound basis for the original project to proceed. Indeed, it is usually good practice for a consultant to be at least thinking, if not working, at a degree of freedom beyond that set by the client's thinking.

For example, a multinational firm was considering reviewing the remuneration packages of its top 200 or so executives. Some worked in subsidiary companies and some at head office, but all were treated for remuneration purposes as a single executive cadre. The consultant looked into the business and personnel policies used by the client and discovered that only rarely did an executive move from one subsidiary to another and the subsidiaries were largely autonomous – they did not depend on one another. The executive cadre was a myth, there was no need for it. Thereafter, each executive was dealt with according to the subsidiary he or she worked for; the only 'executive cadre' was at corporate headquarters. The consultant had, necessarily, extended the scope of the brief to include issues of personnel policy so as to deal with the remuneration review satisfactorily.

This example illustrates the value of thinking at a degree of freedom greater than that of the client. The 'levels of intervention' model described below is a useful framework for doing this.

MAKING SENSE OF A CLIENT'S PREDICAMENT

It has sometimes been said that a consultant decides the answer to the client's problem on Day 2 of the project and spends the rest of the project proving that this is indeed the case. If it proves not to be the case, then he or she goes back again and chooses another answer and checks to see whether that is appropriate.

This type of approach may work with simple problems but it is of limited value when dealing with messy problems. It relies on the consultant's preconceptions, and allows little scope for creativity. By contrast, a consultancy problem solving process for addressing messy problems must recognize that preconceptions inevitably exist and engage with them constructively.

Recognizing preconceptions

It is inevitable that the parties to a consultancy project bring preconceptions that are fashioned by their assumptions. Your judgement about what is relevant in a given situation, for example, will be a function of the skills, knowledge and experience relating to your expertise and its application. Plainly, it is neither possible nor appropriate to try to eliminate expert judgement from consultancy projects. But when entering on any consultancy project – particularly one of any complexity – it is sensible to examine the preconceptions of both consultant and client to see whether they are valid.

For example, a firm of solicitors decided that it wanted to improve the quality of its client service. It therefore engaged consultants to design and run a training course for all staff, which emphasized the importance of good-quality client service and suggested how it might be developed. In the event, the programme failed to improve the quality of client service because of the different preconceptions of the consultants and the solicitors:

- Each had clear, but different, views of what constituted good client service.

- The consultancy had previously provided similar training elsewhere, so assumed that this would be an appropriate method with this firm of solicitors.

- The solicitors took the view that training would be sufficient alone. The consultants failed to challenge this. What was needed in practice, however, was a framework in which people who had received the training could apply it.

Whenever a client and consultant come together, each will have some preconceptions relating to the prospective project. In the example above, consultant and client had similar preconceptions; had these been challenged, a better performance development programme should have resulted.

In other cases, their preconceptions may be different. For example, a consultant may have an idealized view of how a business such as the client's should work and base his or her diagnosis on a comparison of what is going on with that of an ideal. By contrast, the client may see the work required of the consultant entirely in terms of alleviating symptoms.

There are dangers with both perspectives. These can be illustrated by an analogy with a visit to a doctor. Suppose you visit your GP because you have a stomach pain; here, the doctor is in the role

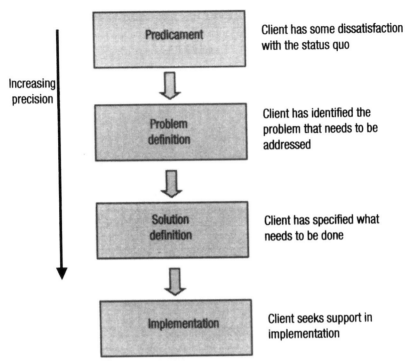

Figure 6.4 Progressive precision of specification

of consultant, and you are the client. Taking an idealized view, the doctor might carry out an examination and say, 'I'm afraid you're a little overweight, and you have some skin blemishes. Your eyesight and hearing are not as good as they might be, and you look pretty unfit.'

All this may be true, but none of it is about your stomach pain. A consultant's diagnosis based on a comparison with an ideal will be equally unhelpful to a client.

On the other hand, you would not think much of a doctor who simply gave you tablets to take away the stomach pain, without bothering to examine you at all. The treatment may alleviate the symptoms, but not deal with the underlying problem. For similar reasons, a consultant should not confine his or her intervention to dealing only with the symptoms a client reports. Of course, as with a visit to a doctor, a client will describe the symptoms at the outset, but these should provide simply the starting point for the consultancy assignment.

So, it is inevitable that both client and consultant will have pre-conceptions about a problem when they start work together. That they are preconceptions does not automatically invalidate them, however. A problem solving process should therefore recognize that preconceptions exist and that they may have value and provide for them to be challenged where necessary.

Developing an understanding of the client's situation

Figure 5.8 in the previous chapter showed the structure by which the thinking of client and consultant could be progressed. This approach is an essential one in developing an understanding of the client's situation; the figure is reproduced above in Figure 6.4 with the addition of a further stage: that of implementation.

There is a structured method to understanding a client's situation, which can be best illustrated by a simple case study: International Cutlery Company (ICC), which is set out below.

John Smith, a consultant, had been invited by the General Manager of the International Cutlery Company to tender for a project for reducing the cost of producing cutlery. 'Our competitors seem to be able to produce it for a lot less than we can – and I want to get our costs down to the same level as theirs', the General Manager explained when Smith met him.

The business was a small subsidiary of Armfather Industries. As he showed Smith round the factory, the General Manager explained what was going on. In one corner, a group of operatives were sitting around laughing and chatting. The General Manager explained, 'They work on the "C" production line; they're having to wait while an engineer fixes the packaging machine.'

Quality control was very interesting; a large number of pieces of cutlery that did not meet specification had been placed in two piles. 'One pile are those which can easily be put right', explained the quality inspector. 'Those others are a dead loss – they could never be fixed.' Smith asked whether the rejects were the result of the week's production so far.

'Goodness, no,' exclaimed the Inspector, 'these are just this morning's.' The General Manager grumbled as they left. 'That means more overtime. Overtime costs are high enough as it is!'

Just as they reached the finishing shop, the General Manager's secretary rushed up to them. 'I'm so glad to have caught you,' she said to him, 'Robinsons are on the line; they want to fix lunch sometime so that they can go over next year's prices with you.'

'I'd better talk to them', said the General Manager. 'Can you excuse me whilst I pop back to my office for five minutes? Robinsons are our major suppliers,' he went on to explain, before he left, 'they produce first class stuff, and their deliveries are always spot on. But, they really charge for it! That meeting is to discuss the price increase they're proposing for next year.'

John Smith went on into the finishing shop with the supervisor who had been hovering in the background since he had walked in with the General Manager. They chatted about the different qualities of finish various customers required. One interesting thing he learned was that most of the specifications had not changed at all over the last five years.

Issue analysis

The first step when faced with the situation described in the case study is to identify what the issues are. An issue can be prefaced with the phrase, 'I'm worried about... '. At the end of his visit, therefore, John Smith might say, based on his observations:

I'm worried about... :

- wastage and rework rates;
- machine downtime;
- operative waiting time;
- customer expectations of quality;
- overtime costs;
- suppliers' prices.

Based on his previous experience, he might add other issues to this list – for example:

I'm worried about... :

- the manning levels;
- work methods used;
- levels of stocks.

None of these last three points can be inferred directly from those given above; John Smith has added them because of his specialized knowledge.

At this stage, these issues are only conjectural; John Smith does not know whether they are substantive or not. For example, by chance he may have arrived on the only day there has been a machine breakdown in five years, and so machine downtime would not be a major cause of uncompetitive productivity. John Smith might also identify issues that are not related to the General Manager's concern with productivity, for example:

I'm worried about:

- the General Manager's secretary interrupting us over a supplier's telephone call;
- the General Manager's response to this interruption;
- the supervisor's speaking only in the absence of the General Manager.

Having created a long list of worries or issues, it is sensible to try to create some sort of structure among them. They are likely to be related in some ways, so a simple method is to cluster them around similar themes. These diagrams in various forms are called mind maps, spidergrams, or cause and effect diagrams. This layout can often stimulate further thoughts and ideas.

This technique is applied to the case study in Figure 6.5, which shows the issues relating to the purpose of improving productivity at ICC.

It shows the purpose (improve productivity) at the centre of the diagram. Around it are shown the issues that have been cited before, which have been grouped according to theme. Issues can appear in more than one place if that seems appropriate; for example, in the diagram, machine downtime appears twice (on the equipment theme and on the systems theme) as a contributory cause of operative waiting time. In practice, the best way of going about this is first to create an unstructured list of issues by brain-storming and then to map them on to the cause and effect diagram as shown. Writing the ideas on the diagram will help to create more ideas about what others might be appropriate. The figure does not show issues outside the General Manager's presenting concern; these could be the subject of a separate diagram and will be a func-tion of deciding where to start and your freedom to do so (see below). As a practical tip, if a consultant team is involved, then it is useful to do this work as a 'case conference', sharing perceptions, understanding and experience.

Remember that issue analysis is not conclusive; a number of these issues identified will be speculative at best and will need further information before they can be validated (or not). So, issue analysis can be a useful pointer to a requirement for further data.

Levels of intervention

The issues identified in the ICC case study are of different moment. For example, 'increase the reliability of the packaging machine on

Figure 6.5 Issues shown on a cause and effect diagram

the "C" production line' and 'replace the General Manger as he is incompetent'. The latter would require a more profound intervention than the former; indeed, it might not be an option.

The notion of 'levels of intervention' enables you to decide the appropriate starting point for a consultancy project. They can be defined as:

1. *Purposes.* The aims that the client has in mind when inviting consultancy help.

2. *Problems.* The problem areas that must be addressed if the purposes are to be achieved.

3. *Solutions.* What the solutions should be.

4. *Implementation.* The plans and activities for resolving the problem by means of the chosen solutions.

After the visit the General Manager (GM) of ICC might call up John Smith saying, 'As you can see, our main problem is the "C" production line. We obviously need to refurbish the equipment, and we'd like you to oversee the project.' A level 4 intervention would be for John Smith to implement the GM's plans and support the refurbishment.

At a level 3 intervention, John Smith would accept the GM's diagnosis of the problem, but might question the solution. He might look for other ways of improving productivity on the 'C' production line – for example, by improved methods, materials flow or planning.

If John Smith intervened at level 2, he might identify other problems that could contribute to high production costs, besides those of the 'C' production line. During his visit, he might note:

- operatives idle while the packaging machine was being fixed;

- large piles of rejects;

- high overtime costs;

- high supplier prices;

- unchanged specifications.

He would need to check whether these are important contributory factors to high production costs. There may be other problems too, which need consideration.

Finally, if John Smith made a level 1 intervention, he would query the General Manager's initial statement of purpose. Is it true that the production costs of his competitors are less? Does the financial structure of the cutlery business mean that ICC can match its competitors? Would it be worthwhile? These are all questions he might ask at this level.

Although we have defined four levels, they are on a continuum. For example, the more precisely a problem becomes defined and understood, the closer you get to a solution. Each level proceeds on the basis of assumptions about the earlier level; for example, if your level of intervention is about formulating solutions, then this will be predicated on assumptions about the nature of the problems that have to be addressed. Similarly, the definition of problems will follow assumptions about purposes – what is to be achieved in the first place.

Going back to the ICC case study example, having identified the levels of intervention John Smith could make, you can see that the intervention at level 4 cited first is based on assumptions about the preceding levels, namely:

- ICC's competitors have a cost advantage and ICC must reduce production costs in order to compete (level 1).

- Improving performance on the 'C' production line will have a worthwhile impact on productivity (level 2).

- Refurbishing the machinery will improve productivity on the 'C' production line (level 3).

- So implementing the GM's refurbishment plans will make ICC more competitive (level 4).

There is a clear correlation between this model of levels of intervention and the model of progressive definition shown in Figure 6.4.

Choosing where to start

All consultants should be aware of this hierarchy of intervention. Part of your expertise should be to judge at which level of intervention it is necessary to start and to guide your clients accordingly. At the start of any involvement with a client (that is, before a project has been defined) you must therefore ask the question: 'Can

I take as read any assumptions about the levels above that at which I am operating, on which my work is predicated? Or is there a piece of work that needs to be done to check these out before I engage in the main piece of work?'

Thinking at a degree of freedom more than that of the client means questioning the assumptions on which a client's construction of any problem is based. For example, a large company decided to make its IT department perform better by insisting that it dealt with all internal 'customers' on a commercial basis. Other departments would then be free to use other sources of IT services if they could be provided more cheaply. The manager of the IT department had considerable misgivings about this. Although there would be short-term cost savings, she believed that in the long term the quality of IT systems and support would fall. She decided to proceed with implementing this proposal, however, and discussed how it might be best accomplished with an outside consultant. The consultant had at this point to choose at what level to intervene. A level 4 intervention would have meant setting up the IT department so that it could function effectively on a commercial basis. With a level 3 intervention (a degree of freedom greater than the client was thinking) the consultant would have looked at other ways in which the IT department could improve its service to other parts of the organization.

In the event, on questioning from the consultant, the manager disclosed her misgivings about this solution. Further probing revealed that the problem was really that internal departments resented the way that IT was costed into their budgets as an overhead, rather than for services received. This meant that alternative solutions – changing the costing system – became more appropriate, and this was the one eventually adopted.

Dealing with clients on these matters has to be handled sensitively to avoid appearing to be extending the scope of an assignment needlessly. On the domestic front, we do not welcome our plumber's help on matters other than plumbing – his advice on our financial affairs, for example, would be intrusive. Similarly, a client may become irritated with a training consultant who tries needlessly to develop a training assignment into matters of corporate strategy. Where a problem is clearly and satisfactorily defined, intervening at level 3, to define solutions, is entirely proper.

Of course, you may well have biases or preferences about where you start on a project. This will be strongly influenced by the type of consultancy in which you specialize. For example:

- A strategy consultant may always start by questioning the purposes of a client (level 1).

- A management consultant may focus on identifying problems (level 2) and recommending how they might be resolved (level 3).

- A technical consultant will help with defining solutions (level 3) and how they might be implemented (level 4).

It is important to recognize these biases because you may be required to work at different levels. For example, an IT consultant may need to clarify problems in order to do the job. Similarly, a strategy consultant may need to follow a project through to detailed implementation. Under these circumstances, the project may be broken into separate phases, each dealing with the question at different levels of intervention.

Phasing

If you start a project with a level 4 intervention, then you can predict with a fair degree of confidence how the project will develop. By contrast, with a level 1 intervention it is more difficult to predict what will happen, as work at subsequent levels will depend on the findings of those preceding. Under these circumstances an iterative approach is appropriate, which breaks the consultancy project down into phases, as shown in Figure 6.6.

The work at each level is best dealt with as a separate phase in a project. This implies that in carrying a project through from clarifying purposes to implementing solutions, there should be at least four phases. If you start at level 3, however, you could manage with just two phases. Each phase, of course, could itself be a project with several stages involved.

The example of ICC can be used to illustrate phasing, as follows. The GM telephones John Smith to say that he's concerned about the competitiveness of ICC, and he believes that production costs need to be reduced. John Smith visits the factory; his visit is reported in the account given earlier in this chapter. Based on his

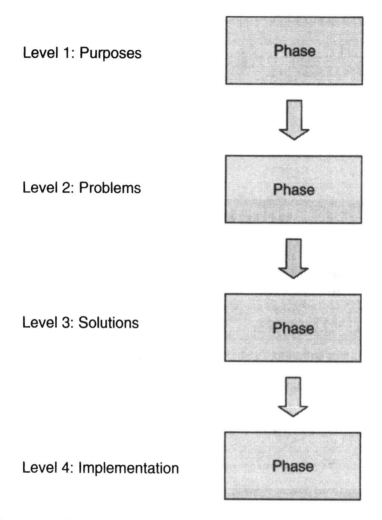

Level 1: Purposes — Phase

Level 2: Problems — Phase

Level 3: Solutions — Phase

Level 4: Implementation — Phase

Figure 6.6 Successive levels of intervention should be treated as different phases of a project

appraisal, John Smith accepts the GM's view of the purposes, and decides to start with a level 2 intervention, identifying the problems that lead to high production costs.

At the end of this phase, John Smith might report to the GM with his appraisal of the issues that must be addressed if ICC's production costs are to be reduced. The GM might then ask, 'What should we do to resolve these issues?' This is a level 3 intervention, which therefore forms the next phase of the project.

When this is complete, John Smith would report to the GM with recommendations on how the issues should be addressed. Finally, the GM might ask John Smith to implement his recommendations (a level 4 intervention).

Of course, you may not be able to start at the level you ideally would like, perhaps because of your level of entry into the client organization, or because of your client's expectations of you. In such a case it may be best to start at a lower level of intervention and seek to understand the situation better as well as providing help to the client. With a better understanding – and a closer relationship with the client – it may then be possible to present your views in a way that the client accepts.

THE PROBLEM SOLVING APPROACH

We have seen that the consultant's first task is to define the questions that need to be answered to resolve the client's predicament and that the idea of 'levels of intervention' can direct attention to the type of questions to be asked. We have also noted that it is helpful to have a process that will enable the questions to be addressed, and this is set out below.

Outline of the approach

We noted earlier that consultants and clients arrive at situations with preconceptions, and these, together with experience and expertise, may provide some promising routes for following up solutions. The problem solving method is one adapted from a method familiar to scientists: that of developing hypotheses, which are then tested through the collection of suitable data.

In what follows, I shall define an *assumption* as valid: it does not need to be checked out. In contrast, I shall define a *hypothesis* as a supposition that is only conjectural, that is, it needs to be checked out before we can accept it. A hypothesis is a contention; some people find it helpful to preface it, like a debating topic, with the words, 'This house believes… ', or even more simply with the word 'perhaps'. An assumption can be taken as read, but a hypothesis needs data collection to verify it. For example, take the statement, 'It is raining'; if it is an assumption, you will take it to be true and

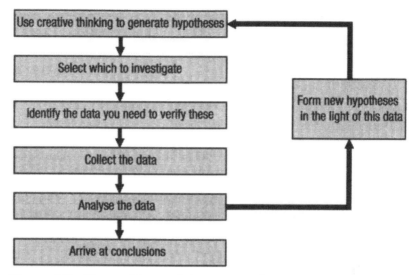

Figure 6.7   The problem solving approach

take an umbrella if you go out. If it is a hypothesis ('Perhaps it is raining') this implies that you are not sure whether it is indeed raining, and may wish to check before taking your umbrella.

The way in which preconceptions can be accommodated is by regarding them as hypotheses; similarly, all the ideas you have at the start of a project can provide fuel for hypotheses. Hypotheses provide a guide to data collection, which is directed towards checking them out. The problem solving approach based on hypotheses is shown in Figure 6.7.

The approach starts with hypotheses, which are generated by creative thinking. This creative stage is followed by an evaluative stage in which you select which hypotheses to investigate. Data collection is directed at verifying these selected hypotheses; during data collection you may also come up with further hypotheses. Finally, you arrive at conclusions. A conclusion can be thought of as a proven hypothesis; conversely a hypothesis can be thought of as a provisional conclusion.

Creative thinking in consultancy

Creative thinking was mentioned in the previous section as a method of creating hypotheses. If there is a characteristic that distinguishes excellent consultants from the merely good, it is that of creativity. One consultant defines creativity as, 'that which is obvious only in retrospect'. My own experience endorses this when working with a colleague or client, whose insight provides the key to finding the way forward in resolving a problem. Or, in my own work, having struggled with defining a way forward, stumbling on the key and reflecting, 'Why on earth didn't I think of that before – it seems so obvious (now!).'

People are naturally creative but are often educated out of it. One has only to look at a group of children playing anywhere in the world to realize that creativity is an innate human characteristic. As an adult, to become more creative you must reduce the barriers to creativity. Roger von Oech in his book *A Whack on the Side of the Head* (1990) identifies ten barriers to creative thinking. They are shown below:

The right answer	That's not logical
Follow the rules	Be practical
Avoid ambiguity	To err is wrong
Play is frivolous	That is not my area
Don't be foolish	I am not creative

All these rules are appropriate at some time or another. For example, we may not be very enthusiastic to hear a surgeon describe the operation he is about to carry out on us as outside his specialization, or that he might be experimenting with a new technique that has a high risk of failure compared with other ones that he might use. Similarly, we do not want our bankers to be using our money in risky and creative ways if it means that we might lose it. Creativity, therefore, has to be applied appropriately. There is a time to be creative, using divergent thinking; there is a time to be analytical, evaluating the ideas created.

Typically, though, people working in groups mix creative and evaluative thinking. Someone will come up with an idea, which will then be evaluated by the whole group. (Sometimes evaluation consists in completely overlooking it!) The process that is being used is that of creating an idea and then evaluating it, repeating the process as required.

This process of cycling between creative thinking and then evaluative thinking inhibits creativity. Many of the 'barriers to creativity' quoted above are quite appropriate when engaged in evaluative thinking. When engaging in mixed thinking, sometimes the barriers will be in place, some of the time they will be suspended. The problem for a participant in a problem solving meeting is discerning whether they are in place or suspended; the safe bet is to assume that they are in place. What therefore happens is that evaluative thinking takes over and few ideas are created.

A useful method of dealing with this difficulty is to separate the idea creation process from that of evaluation, into two explicit stages. First you generate lots of ideas, and then only after you have finished this stage do you pick out the ones that merit further investigation. This latter process of separated thinking is used in brainstorming techniques. In brainstorming there is a creative period, where the aim is to create a large quantity of ideas – not quality, because quality implies evaluation. Evaluation is suspended until a later analytical period.

Techniques for creating ideas

The classic approach to brainstorming suggests various techniques for generating ideas. One such is 'freewheeling' – just noting ideas as they pop into your head. Another is (when working in a group) to let an idea suggested by one person stimulate others.

Both these techniques, however, start with some notion of the idea under consideration and move on from there. An alternative technique is to start from 'somewhere completely different' and see whether that gives you new insights. For instance, you could start with a completely random set of words, and see how they might relate to the problem under consideration. (Sometimes this is known as 'random entry technique'.) Take a few of the words that have been used in the last few pages:

working	random
motion	completely
alternatives	struggled

Consider the problem quoted above of improving performance at International Cutlery Company. You would then try to see if any of the words above might provide an insight that you previously had not considered. What relationship might there be, for example, between 'struggled' and 'improving performance'? Setting a group

Level	Assumptions	Hypotheses
1	There is a predicament that merits attention	What purposes this implies
2	The purposes to be achieved	The problems that stand in the way of achieving this purpose
3	The problems that must be addressed	How they might be resolved
4	The solutions that must be put in place	How they might best be implemented

Figure 6.8   Assumptions and hypotheses at each level of intervention

exercise where operations are challenged to find ways of improving performance might be an idea linking the two.

Another technique is to use metaphor or analogy; for example, what insights can we get if this problem is thought of as a water distribution system? A piece of music? A meal? And there are other techniques, covered in many books. Simon Majaro's 1988 book *The Creative Gap* is to be particularly recommended. The first step in the technique is to develop hypotheses; these should vary according to the level of intervention. Figure 6.8 shows the assumptions and hypotheses for each level.

Points to note are:

- Hypotheses at a given level of intervention are related to the outputs for that level.

- The hypotheses for one level are assumptions for the next, hence each level should be dealt with as a separate phase.

- If your thinking is to be 'one degree of freedom more than that of the client', then what you do is to treat the client's assumptions as hypotheses.

To illustrate these processes we will again refer to the International Cutlery Company case study set out above. Assume that at the end of his visit, John Smith, the consultant, has decided to accept the GM's stated purpose of improving productivity so there is no need for intervention at level 1. This purpose therefore is the assumption underlying level 2, and so John Smith would start at this level by using creative thinking to develop hypotheses about the issues that relate to low productivity. He would derive these hypotheses from his observations during his visit, his knowledge and previous experience and his imagination.

John Smith may, of course, have created ideas that are not hypotheses about issues, but relate to other levels of intervention; for example, 'The GM is useless and should be fired.' This is a hypothesis about a solution; it is appropriate for level 3, but not for level 2 at which John Smith is currently working. He can use it, though, to identify further problems by asking, 'To what problem would this solution relate?' This solution is about 'the quality of management', so he could add 'quality of management' as a further problem he might investigate.

Practical hints in defining hypotheses

Some practical tips in carrying out this process follow. If you are working in a group in developing ideas, it is common to use a flip chart to record them. When they are coming thick and fast, it is difficult for whoever is doing the writing to get down all the detail. In such circumstances, it is usual practice to abbreviate or to abstract the ideas. This is a dangerous practice. By abstraction or abbreviation, much of the richness of the ideas is lost and where they are expressed imprecisely, it becomes very difficult to verify them (as we shall see when we come to looking at data collection).

Sometimes the reverse is the case. When recording ideas during a creative session, those responsible for writing them down often behave as if ink was highly expensive! So write down all the ideas and then evaluate them; if the scribe acts as editor, it means that the evaluation is happening prematurely. Don't worry if you have some ideas that appear totally irrelevant during the initial trawl for them; they can be edited out later.

Following up every hypothesis is not practical or necessary, so some process of hypothesis selection is required. This is where you have to exercise your judgement, based on your expertise. The stages involved in selecting which hypotheses are to be pursued are as follows:

1. Disregard those hypotheses that are not relevant to the issues being studied. If the process of hypothesis creation has been dealt with properly, lots of ideas will have been recorded that have very little relevance to the scope of the project. By a process of inspection, disregard those that seem completely irrelevant. If in doubt, leave the ideas in.

2. Assess the remainder according to their relevance and probability. For example at ICC, salespeople's motivation may be an issue, but it does not appear immediately relevant to the purpose of increasing productivity. John Smith may also have hypothesised that, 'Competing manufacturers are engaged in sabotage.' This is improbable, so again it is one that would not be pursued as a matter of priority.

3. Hypotheses should be then classified into three categories:

   – A   Those that must be investigated because they are of central importance.
   – C   Those that could be investigated, but only if there was time. (The missing category, B, is for those that you are unsure whether to put into category A or C.)

After this process, you should have a shortlist of hypotheses that you are going to follow up through the process of data collection. It is a good idea at this point to take stock of your list of hypotheses; do they seem sufficient to you?

This is a sort of reality test; if you feel that having gone through this process you would still want to explore some items outside those hypotheses, it usually means that there is a hypothesis that you have not yet articulated. If you feel unhappy, therefore, think carefully through what you have done so far. Is there anything missing from the logic? If so, what is it?

DATA COLLECTION

The problem solving method is about taking a structured approach to understanding a client's predicament. We saw, however, that there are some areas where you can confidently assume the correctness of your views while in others they should be regarded as hypothetical or speculative.

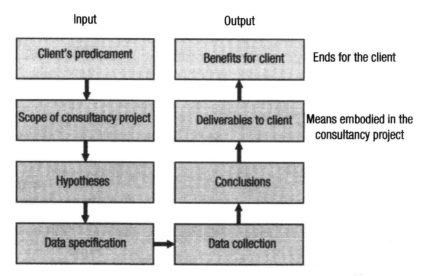

Figure 6.9 The problem solving approach as an input–output model

Figure 6.7 shows the stages involved. Data collection is shown as a means by which you can test hypotheses, proving them to be true or false or at least shedding a little light on them. But we should never lose sight of the fact that consultancy projects are a means to an end, that end being to the benefit of the client. So, the figure can be redrawn as an input–output model, as shown in Figure 6.9. The scope of the consultancy project will determine the nature of the deliverables to the client. Hypotheses can be regarded as provisional conclusions, while conclusions can be regarded as proven hypotheses. The data that is collected will be a function of the data specification. So there is a symmetry about inputs and outputs as well as the sequence shown in Figure 6.7. Data collection is key to this process.

There are two essential considerations in data collection: defining what data is required; and using an appropriate method to gather it.

Defining what data is required

Data collection is a time-consuming element in any consultancy project and so one of the most expensive. It is essential that you are clear about what data you are aiming to collect and why you are doing so. It is very easy for the intellectually curious to go along some cul-de-sacs and expensively collect data that has little relevance to the questions in hand. The process of data collection should therefore be directed to verifying the hypotheses that you have selected.

On this basis, you could produce a specification of what data is required, and then go out and collect it. In practice, consultancy requires more. One feature of first engaging with a new client or assignment is the process of familiarization. The consultant has to get to know the client – the people, the culture, the business processes, etc – and the client has to learn how to accommodate the consultant and the project being undertaken. Each is progressing along a learning curve about the other, and it is unusual for familiarization to be embodied in a formal process of data collection.

Figure 6.10 shows how the scope of a project evolves and the nature of data collection that goes along with it. Early in the project, you need to develop a feel for the political environment in the client. Data collection therefore is open-ended, and you will be concerned with opinions as much as facts. Next, you will generate and revise hypotheses during this scoping and familiarization phase (it is worth noting that you may wish to revise your hypotheses as a result of data collection). Once you have established your shortlist of hypotheses, then your data collection can become more focused on the data you need to check out your selected hypotheses.

Data collection can be of two broad kinds: 1) open-ended, where you cannot be precise about what it is you need to know; and 2) close-ended, where you know exactly what you need to find out. As shown in Figure 6.10, open-ended data collection is more appropriate during the early stages of a project.

Open-ended data specification

Here it is useful to create an exploratory agenda. Typically, it will consist of areas of interest of enquiry that you want to explore, with perhaps subsidiary topics that you want specifically to look at.

The specification can be generated simply from the sort of cause and effect analysis shown in Figure 6.5. The main legs of the diagram could provide the areas of enquiry, the branches

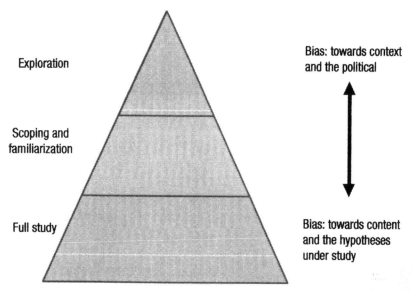

Figure 6.10   Data collection evolves with the project

from them could point towards the topics that you want information on. So, the data specification could appear as in Figure 6.11 below.

In this example, taken from the International Cutlery Company case study, each of the topics relates to an issue that John Smith may want to explore in more detail.

What often happens is that information gathered in the early exploratory stages prompts new ideas of what data is important to collect and the data specification is modified accordingly.

Close-ended data specification

When engaged in close-ended data collection, you can specify more precisely:

- what data you need;
- what form it might take – for example, what units it is measured in;
- where you might find it.

Specifying precisely what data you need becomes particularly important when working in teams of consultants; each member of

Area of enquiry	Topic
1. Systems	1.1 Operative waiting time
	1.2 Machine downtime
	1.3 Wastage and rework rates
	1.4 Method
2. Equipment	2.1 Machine downtime
3. Materials	3.1 Supplies prices
	3.2 Stock levels
	3.3 Customer expectations of quality
4. People	4.1 Manning levels
	4.2 Downtime costs

Figure 6.11 Open-ended data specification

the team must be clear what data he or she has to collect. For example, a multi-country study would be of little use if the information from each country was not compatible, because different consultants had interpreted what was required in different ways.

To illustrate the process of data specification, we will again consider the ICC case study, but at a level 3 intervention – one at which the issues have been confirmed and the work now consists of identifying how best they might be addressed.

Suppose that the issue John Smith is to investigate is that of overtime costs, and that he has selected hypotheses for the problems underlying this issue as follows:

- There is too much work for the labour force.

- People are not working hard enough.

- People are not sufficiently skilled.

- Work is poorly planned.

- Overtime pay rates are high.

Practice differs in consultancies in how they set out a data specification. Some consultancies identify what is called a 'key question related to each hypothesis'. This is a question, which if answered, would help you to judge whether the hypothesis is true.

The perfect question would simply be an inversion of the hypothesis: thus in the list of hypotheses quoted above, the hypothesis 'too much work for the labour force' would invite the key question 'Is there too much work for the labour force?' Indeed, some consultancies do not distinguish between hypotheses and key questions – confusingly, they call them all 'questions'. I prefer the split into hypotheses and key questions, as a key question can be phrased to illuminate one part of a hypothesis.

Key questions are particularly helpful if the hypothesis is expressed very generally and has to be focused before any work can be done in investigating whether it is true. This depends on the degree of abstraction of an idea. An example of increasing degrees of abstraction are as follows:

- Spot is a small, playful, furry thing.

- Spot is a puppy.

- A puppy is a pet.

- A pet is an animal.

'Spot' is a specific, concrete idea; 'animal' is far more general and abstract. A hypothesis about Spot will be easier to verify than one about animals in general. The 'key question' technique can therefore be used to help to reduce the degree of abstraction of a hypothesis. In the ICC case study, for example, you might come up with the hypothesis 'quality is poor'. This is abstract and difficult to verify, but could be made more concrete through key questions such as:

- Are wastage rates above the industry average?

- Do customers return goods as being of inadequate quality?

- Are quality standards set too high?

Once the key question has been phrased, a data specification can be prepared. A data specification defines:

- what data is required;

- what format it might be in;

- where it might be found.

Data	Format	Sources	Checks
Current pay in ICC for overtime	Hourly rates, basis of variation	Personnel department	
Current distribution of overtime earnings	By grade, dept., job category	Personnel department	Do these reconcile?
Any local or industry agreements	Terms of agreement	Personnel department	
What local companies are comparable	List of likely competitors for labour	Local Chamber of Commerce	ICC Personnel dept
What overtime rates are paid in those companies	Same format as ICC	Company personnel department	Recruitment agencies

Figure 6.12   Close-ended data specification

The data specification also shows checks: where there is a particularly crucial piece of data that is required, you may wish to have more than one source of it. Figure 6.12 shows a completed data specification for collecting information about International Cutlery Company's overtime costs and how they compare with those elsewhere.

Compromise is often necessary

Data is expensive to collect, in terms of time, and thus in money. Often you have to determine what data is necessary and sufficient, and then possibly to compromise still further. The need for compromise is raised here, because hard data is sometimes difficult or impossible to collect. For example, it may be desirable to know the market prices of each supplier of widgets across the world, but official statistics may not cover this, and the manufacturers themselves could be reluctant to provide them to you. Alternatively, you could be subject to disinformation. A compromise may be made by substituting qualitative for quantitative data, and opinion or consensus in the absence of objective data.

The latter is particularly necessary with soft data – that relating, for example, to views and opinions. Soft data is important when dealing with recommendations or matters of implementation, when recognition of the political climate, and the culture and values of an organization, may be essential in achieving acceptance. The more senior your client, the more likely he or she is to be concerned about soft issues and data, such as those concerning competitiveness, communication and morale.

Choosing a method of data collection

There are four generic methods of collecting data:

● face to face from other people;

● remotely from other people, by using questionnaires or similar documents;

● looking at documents and records;

● direct observation.

Each has its pros and cons, which are summarized in Figure 6.13.

Pros and cons of different methods of data collection

Quite apart from their intrinsic merits, when you have to choose a method for collecting the data you need, there are four other criteria to be met:

1. Is it sufficiently open-ended? Will it collect the data required on the hypotheses being explored? It is important that wrong assumptions are not built in (for example, as in the question 'When did you stop beating your wife?')

2. Will it collect the 'soft data' required? This relates to people's opinions. These will be particularly important in considering the acceptability (or otherwise) of recommendations, for example. Hard data leads to idealistic solutions; soft data provides information on how to make them workable and acceptable.

3. What will its impact be? Remember that data collection is an intervention into an organization. This, if poorly handled, can have dysfunctional effects. On the other hand, the data

Method of data collection	Pros	Cons
Interviews one to one	Personal contact with the interviewee	Time-consuming
	Unstructured – you can follow up points of interest	Difficult to decide who to see
	The interviewee has made a clear contribution	Time-consuming to analyse
	Enables you to judge what sort of person the interviewee is	
Interviews one with a group	You can meet more people	Hard work – probably needs two people
	The project has a higher profile	Less opportunity for individuals to contribute
		People may be inhibited from contributing
Questionnaires	You can collect a large number of views	Close-ended; you get answers only to the questions you ask
	A well-designed questionnaire should be easy to analyse	Must be self-explanatory
	The respondent can fill in as and when he or she wants	Respondents may have reservations about committing their views to writing
	Is not time-consuming for client staff	No sense of strength of feeling or relevance (although you can put in scales to test this)
		Low response rates
Document inspection	Good chance of getting unexpected data	Limited availability of documentation
	You can go at your own rate	Time-consuming for consultant
		Can be difficult to find the data wanted
Observation	First-hand information	Observation can affect the system being observed
	Good chance of picking up something unexpected	Time-consuming
		Difficult to analyse

Figure 6.13 Pros and cons of different methods of data collection

collection method can be used to suggest processes of desirable change, or to give the project a suitable profile in the organization.

4. Is it economical and effective?

Finally, remember that as data collection is itself an intervention into the client's organization, it is not possible for you to carry it out without in some way affecting the views of the client's staff about you, your practice and the project you are undertaking. A well-constructed and executed data collection plan can enhance your credibility, yield high-quality solutions and help to ensure more ready acceptance of your recommendations.

Interviewing skills

Much of the data will be collected using interviews. Your interview plan should reflect the type of data that you require to answer the key questions related to your hypotheses. Bear in mind that you could have objectives for the meeting other than data collection, such as:

- building relationships with the interviewee;
- giving information;
- canvassing support for a particular view or opinion;
- problem solving;
- decision making.

Remember to leave sufficient time in the programme for data analysis as well as collection; for example, to write up or consolidate interview notes and to relate the data to your hypotheses. Interviewing requires sustained concentration and is tiring, so do not try to pack in too many interviews in a short time. A good rule of thumb is to allocate twice as much time to an interview programme as the time you expect to spend face to face with interviewers. Try to structure data collection in a logical order so that key questions are answered first, and so that you avoid carrying out data collection that subsequently proves needless. Aim to get the data with the greatest 'leverage' first. For example, if the support of a Managing Director is crucial to the acceptance of your proposals, you need to find out if he or she has any strong dislikes or preferences fairly quickly, and this could condition which hypotheses you select to pursue.

DATA ANALYSIS AND CONCLUSIONS

The data collection process accumulates facts, which then have to be processed to produce conclusions. Ideally, what should have happened is that the case for or against each hypothesis should have been made. A proven hypothesis is a conclusion, and so the conclusions from a full study would be a list of the hypotheses that had been proven.

Consultancy is more expedient than science and so, sadly, rarely as rigorous as this. The whole process is a little more messy. Nonetheless, it is essential that your conclusions stand up to examination, like the layers of skin in an onion. Peeling away the top layer shows another layer as fine as the first; peeling the second layer away reveals a third, and so on. So too should it be with a consultant's thinking. For example, it is said of a former chief executive of an international firm that if you went to him with a proposal, he would take one part of your case, and ask 'Why?' of it. He would then take an aspect of your answer, and ask 'Why?' of that. He would then ask 'Why?' of an aspect of your next answer. If you could answer these three layers of questions satisfactorily, he would accept that you had thought through your case.

Three layers of thinking can be thought of in data analysis:

- Data – the facts you have collected.

- Findings – an evaluation of these facts. (This usually relies on unspecified data, such as a standard or normal practice.)

- Conclusions – the diagnosis drawn from the evaluation.

The interventions that are required to address the areas of concern can then be specified according to the conclusions. Interventions are of varying kinds; frequently they consist of recommendations for the client's action, but they might also be action by the consultant, such as:

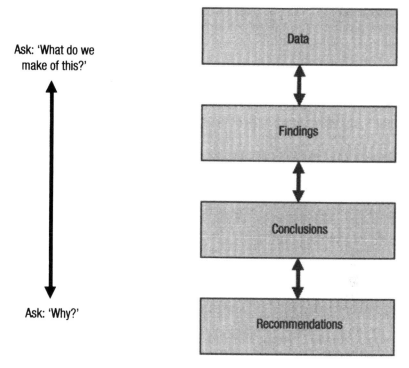

Ask: 'What do we
make of this?'

Ask: 'Why?'

Figure 6.14   From data to recommendations

- training client staff;
- conducting a further project;
- taking an executive role;
- supporting the work of an individual or group.

For example:

- It is raining (a piece of data).
- The weather is bad (finding). (This is evaluative because the rain may not be bad for a farmer whose crops need rain; the unspecified piece of data is that we want the weather to be fine.)
- We cannot go for a picnic (conclusion).
- We should eat lunch indoors (recommendation).

Figure 6.14 shows the relationships:

- Data lead to findings.

- Findings draw you to conclusions.

- The specification of the intervention(s) is based on conclusions.

Each step leads to the next by asking, 'What do we make of this, with respect to the topics we are examining?' Also, the logic can be tested in reverse by asking, 'Why – what leads us to this view?' Of course, in practice the process of splitting data, findings and conclusions under the headings shown can be a messy process. You can have difficulty sorting out what is a piece of data, a finding or a conclusion. A practical technique for dealing with this ambiguity is:

1. Divide a large piece of newsprint/flip chart paper into three columns, headed 'Data', 'Findings', 'Conclusions'.

2. Write your data, findings and conclusions on 'Post It' or similar type labels.

3. Stick them under the appropriate headings and inspect to see whether they are correctly allocated.

Use of these labels means that you can move a comment from one heading to another. A major criterion to use is that they all fit together. Once you are happy you have allocated your labels correctly, you should ask the following questions of your analysis:

1. Does the data lead logically to the findings and the findings to the conclusions? In particular, are there any alternative interpretations that could be made at any stage?

2. Are there key findings that have not been substantiated, which could be used to corroborate the conclusions?

3. Do the findings rest crucially on a narrow range of data? What would be the result if this data were inaccurate, and how inaccurate would it have to be before you changed your conclusions? How likely is it to be inaccurate? Thus the links between the various stages are tested.

There remains the final and most important test, which is to refer back to the assignment objectives:

4. Will the interventions specified satisfactorily address the areas of concern put to us? Have we met our commitments to

producing outputs? Will our conclusions form a sufficient basis to move the project ahead?

The assignment objectives should be held in mind throughout the project. It is easy to stray away from the original objectives and specify interventions that, although totally logical and valid, fail to meet the client's original concerns. Remember to reread your original proposal regularly during the project.

7

Commercial aspects of consultancy

If a consultancy firm is to be viable, it must generate revenue. The bulk of income will come from charging fees to clients and so in this chapter we start by considering how these might be determined.

DETERMINING FEE RATES

For the most part the fees charged to a client will be related to the cost of the project, the cost being primarily that of the time spent on it by the consultants in the project team. (Other methods of generating revenue in a consultancy practice are dealt with in a later section.) The cost of the time is usually based on a daily fee rate; the level of fee rate required can be calculated as follows.

At the start of Chapter 4, we considered a consultancy firm that had 25 consultants paid on average £40,000 per annum. The fully absorbed on-costs and overheads were assumed to be as much again, resulting in total costs of £2 million per annum. If average utilization on fees (days on fees divided by paid days) is 60 per cent, the number of fee days in which this has to be recovered is:

60% (utilization) × 260 (days per year) × 25 (no of consultants) = 3900

Break-even fee rate (the fee level required to recover costs) is therefore:

= £2m/3900 = £513 per day

As the consultancy would also need to make a profit, the budgeted fee rate would need to exceed this, so a budgeted fee rate of, say, £600 per day might be set. This would have to be compared with market rates; if this fee rate is markedly greater, then it may mean that overhead costs have to be reduced, so that the fee rate can be cut.

Consultancies frequently charge different fee rates for different grades of consultant. These can be calculated based on individual salaries, as follows. Using the same example from above, the average annual fee income to be generated by a single consultant is:

60% (utilization) × 260 (days per year) × £600 (fee rate) = £93,600 p.a.

The ratio of average fee income to average salary is:

£93,600/£40,000 = 2.34

In practice, among medium- and large-sized practices (with larger overheads) this ratio might be twice as much. Someone earning £30,000 per annum would therefore be expected to generate (2.34 × £30,000 per annum =) £70,200 revenue, and their fee rate would be set accordingly. More usual, however, is to allocate consultants to grades according to their experience, skill and responsibilities, and to set a different fee rate for each grade.

Reductions in fee rate

There are circumstances when reducing fee rates may be appropriate, such as when a contract offers the opportunity to assign a team of consultants for a long period without interruption. Consultancy managers like large contracts, because as a rule, the cost of selling is a smaller percentage of revenue and because long assignments mean fewer gaps between assignments, when consultants might not be earning fees. Both these points mean that the utilization in a consultancy becomes potentially greater when large jobs are being done.

Returning to the example quoted earlier in this chapter: suppose the benefit of changing the sales mix, so that most work consisted of long consultancy assignments, was to increase utilization from 60 per cent to 65 per cent. The revenue would be increased thus:

revenue = 65% (utilization) × 260 (days) × £600 (daily fee rate) × 25 (number of consultants) = £2,535,000

This is an increase of about 8 per cent from that where utilization is 60 per cent. A client, recognizing the benefits of a long assignment, may use this as a negotiating ploy to win a reduction in fee rate. In theory, the consultancy could drop its fee rate by 8 per cent (from £600 per day to £550 per day) and maintain its former revenue. In practice, of course, the decision is rarely arithmetically so precise. The decision to discount will depend on:

- how much you want the work;
- the commercial context – for example, to discourage a competitor winning the work with a long-term, profitable client;
- your relationship with the client;
- what's happening in the rest of the market;
- whether you believe you will lose the assignment if you don't discount.

During a recession, consultancies have been known to discount very heavily to get business. Apart from generating a contribution to fixed costs, the reasons for so doing include wishing to get a toehold in a new client, with the hope of identifying and selling extension work and wanting to keep the consultancy team engaged. Consultants need to be kept busy!

EXPENSES

There are other costs that will come under the heading of expenses, and for which the client will need to budget. Value added tax (VAT) may need to be added to the bill. This is a matter of little contention when the client is subject to VAT, but will represent a real additional cost if the client cannot set it against the VAT on their own business outputs (as with some government departments).

There may be bought-in resources needed to carry out the assignment. These can include:

- specialist equipment;
- software;
- specialist advice or subcontractors;
- purchase of licences.

The need for these will depend on the nature of the assignment. On most assignments, however, travel, subsistence and accommodation expenses will be incurred. When an assignment entails travel to a number of locations, particularly if long distances and overnight accommodation are involved, these can quickly mount up.

Consultancy practices usually have rules governing travel costs (mileage rate for cars, class of travel by train or plane, use of taxis and hired cars), accommodation (grade of hotel) and subsistence (for example, a daily rate). These can provide the basis for estimating the likely expenses under this heading. For example, in the week that I write, I have just had to arrange a short interview programme with a client, which involves travel to locations in London, Bristol and Manchester, and we have agreed a budget as follows:

- London: no charge as close to head office;
- Bristol: travel by car, at an agreed mileage rate;
- Manchester: travel to Heathrow by car; shuttle by air to Manchester; taxi to Manchester centre, and return.

Although this is a trivial example, estimates of expenses on larger jobs can be built up in a similar way. It is worth establishing what the client's rules are for their own employees incurring expenses. For example, a client may baulk at paying for business class flights for consultants when the rules for their own staff state economy.

There may be other expenses related to in-house costs, such as typing or printing. For the treatment of these, see below under 'Non-time-related charges'.

WHAT DO WE TELL THE CLIENT?

Having estimated what the likely costs are on an assignment, what do you agree with the client? The Institute of Management Consultancy has provided some helpful guidance:

There must be a clear understanding between client and consultant:

- as to the objective of the assignment;
- the fees or the basis of fees to be charged.

So besides defining appropriate terms of reference, a consultant's proposal should quote:

- a fixed fee, or;
- a range within which the fee will fall, or;
- the fee rate(s) to be charged in terms of time (hour, day, week) or other defined basis, or;
- (recruitment work) a percentage of emoluments of appointee (with careful definition as necessary of 'emoluments'), any minimum fee or other conditions.

When significant expenses are likely to arise for the client's account some explanation or estimate should be given.

Some contracts are on a 'time and materials' basis: the consultancy keeps a record of the time spent on the assignment, and the related expenses, and charges the client accordingly. The consultant may give an indication of the likely total costs, but is not bound by that. The time and materials basis is used infrequently in management consultancy; it still pertains, however, in other professions (for example, among lawyers on domestic matters).

Most contracts, therefore, are not on a time and materials basis, so you have to tell the client how much the total costs are likely to be to achieve the deliverables required. This estimate is expected to be reasonably binding; the client will not expect you to charge more than the price stated without good cause. The reason for this is simple; most organizations have a budgeting system that requires budget holders to predict likely expenses. If a manager has authority to spend, say, £30,000 on a consultancy project, it can be politically embarrassing for him or her to feel obliged to ask for £10,000 more because the consultants had underestimated the cost of the assignment.

One way of avoiding this is to add a 'contingency' to your estimate, for example, to tell the client to budget for the cost of 20 days' fees when you estimate the project will need only 17. This has the advantage that the client will either be charged less, or get more for his or her money, than expected. (Or, if you are cynical, the consultant will take longer to do the same job, or the consultancy will make more profit!) But even if you add a contingency factor, there is the question, how much should it be? A small contingency will allow for minor errors or alterations to the assignment programme, but will not cover a large misjudgement of the amount of time required. Note that the purpose of a contingency is to cope with underestimates of the amount of work required to carry out a particular project – not to cover changes in the terms of reference (dealt with in Chapter 8).

For the consultancy, therefore, the question is one of managing risk. Furthermore, if there is keen price competition for winning an assignment, the consultancy has to balance the need to keep the price low versus the risk of not allowing enough time to do the work.

This difficulty is compounded when dealing with multi-phase assignments. For example, in the ICC case study (see Chapter 6), John Smith is first going to diagnose what are the major issues leading to high production costs. The next phase will be to address those issues. Although John Smith can estimate with some accuracy the amount of work involved in the first phase, that involved in the next will depend on what he finds out during this diagnosis. It is therefore difficult to estimate how much work would be involved in the second phase before the first is completed. Nonetheless, his client, the General Manager, will probably want an idea of the likely costs of the total project. Not unreasonably so; John Smith might ask for, say, £9,000 to do the first stage of the work, but this is only the start of meeting the client's objective. The GM will want to know what the next stage is likely to cost. Is it going to be £10,000 or £100,000?

So, you are faced with a 'Catch 22' situation: you cannot start the work unless you provide an estimate for the whole project, and you cannot provide a precise estimate until you have started the project. There are three techniques that help to resolve this dilemma:

1. Make explicit the assumptions on which your fee estimate is based. If, for example, you are carrying out data collection by interview, then list the locations at which you will be carrying out the interviews and how many people you expect to see at each. If the client then wants you to see more people, or visit other locations, this is a clear departure from the terms of reference, which invites an adjustment to the fee estimate.

2. A similar approach can be used for estimating (as yet undefined) future phases of work. You could identify one or two likely scenarios that might emerge after the diagnostic phase, and indicate the consultancy costs that would be involved in dealing with these. Again, if you have made your assumptions explicit, findings that depart from these will provide the basis for amending the fee estimate.

3. Quote a fee range. Unless you are undertaking a 'Royal Road' type assignment, the amount of time required to carry out an assignment is not totally predictable. Telling a client that an assignment will take 21 days implies a degree of precision that is usually spurious. If you say it will take (say) 19 to 23 days, this shows that at this stage it is difficult to be precise. As the assignment progresses, you can tell the client where in this range the out-turn is expected to be.

Above all, with fees, as with all other aspects of the client relationship, the consultant should manage clients' expectations. 'No surprises' is a good motto.

TERMS OF PAYMENT

The financial structure of a typical consultancy practice is that although revenue is dependent on sales volume, costs are largely fixed. Costs arise mainly from employee costs and office overheads such as premises. Such a financial structure means that cash flow has to be rigorously controlled. Take, for example, John Smith's practice, where a consultant costs an average of £80,000 per annum with fully absorbed costs. Assume John Smith starts work on 1 May on a three-month assignment, which is completed satisfactorily on 31 July. If he has worked 62 days at £600 per day in this period, the fees will be £37,200, against costs of £20,000 (being the cost related to three months of his time). The profit of £17,200 is healthy. The cash flow may not be, though. Suppose the consultancy submits an invoice for the fees on 15 August. The client may have a system that pays the invoice at the end of the month following that of submission. This invoice will then be paid on 30 September, and the consultancy receives the amount a few days later. The consultancy has therefore had to bear the cost of an increasing amount of work in progress while the assignment was being carried out and the full cost of the assignment for two months while raising the invoice and waiting for it to be paid.

If this is replicated across the practice, there will need to be a large amount of working capital, which will add to the costs of the business. It is therefore important to keep work in progress and debtors low, and this starts with the terms of payment, included in the terms of business.

Because of the time lag in the example given above, consultancies like to have payment on account, or interim payments, for an assignment. These will be against the fees agreed, but the fact that they are made before the end of the assignment will help improve cash flow. The aim is to transfer 'work in progress' to 'debtors' quickly.

In an ideal world, a client would pay for an assignment on commissioning it. This would be marvellous for the consultancy's cash flow, but bad for the client's. Clients are (for the most part) also subject to the same cash flow considerations as the consultancy firm; from the client's point of view, their cash flow would be considerably enhanced by deferring payment until well after the completion of a consultancy project. There has to be a compromise. The client might make stage payments throughout an assignment, perhaps at significant milestones. For example, a recruitment consultant might be paid as follows:

● one-third of the fee at the start of the assignment;

● one-third on presentation of a shortlist of candidates;

● one-third on the position being filled.

Month	Days on fees	Amount (£) invoiced
May	19	11,400
June	21	12,600
July	22	13,200
Total	**62**	**37,200**

Figure 7.1   Invoicing schedule

Whenever there are interim payments, consultants should try to ensure that invoices coincide with the client receiving some value, as in the above example, or on submission of a report, or the completion of a phase of a project. Fees might also be charged according to the time spent by consultants each month. In the example given above, the invoicing schedule might be as shown in Figure 7.1.

Some firms on major projects might invoice more frequently – perhaps on a weekly basis. Whatever the basis of invoicing, this should be agreed with the client and summarized in the terms of business.

Credit terms

The other major factor affecting cash flow is the time lapse between the client receiving an invoice and paying it. Businesses often have payment systems that classify accounts payable into categories of payment at (say) 7 days, 30 days, 60 days, 90 days. Unless the consultancy insists otherwise, the client will put the account payable into the category that offers maximum credit, so the credit period should be agreed and specified in the terms of business.

Payment can be deferred if there is a query on an invoice. Businesses seeking to improve their cash flow may excuse non-payment because 'we have a query on the invoice', whether or not there are grounds for query. Here the consultancy practice might agree with the client at the outset that queries must be raised within a given time after the invoice has been received, otherwise the invoice will be regarded as acceptable.

A consultancy's own procedures can also result in high levels of working capital being required. For example, in one practice, invoices for the month were raised by the sixteenth of the following month. These were then sent to consultants for onward transmission to their clients. Because of queries, consultants being out of the office, and this task being given a low priority compared with selling and operating, it often took as long as a further month before the invoices were sent out. This resulted in high levels of work in progress and debtors. The situation was resolved by the invoices being sent out without approval, direct from the accounts department to the client, but on an agreed basis for each assignment.

The final building block in keeping working capital requirements down is credit control. Consultancies should have a system for chasing up invoices due, but not yet paid.

Cancellation charges

A consultancy can incur expense if a project is cancelled or postponed by a client, particularly at short notice. For example, if a consultancy has reserved two consultants to run a three-day interview programme next week, which the client then postpones, it is usually difficult to find fee earning work at such short notice to fill their time. Even if the consultancy work is carried out at a later date, the six consultant days next week will have been lost.

Under these circumstances, a consultancy practice may seek redress by having a cancellation clause in the contract. This is particularly appropriate when running short projects or training courses, which tend to be one-off events. Obviously, whether the cancellation charge is levied will be subject to wider considerations of the client relationship. Part of the value of a cancellation or postponement clause is, however, that it can restrain clients from changing a programme needlessly – it becomes more worthwhile for them to put themselves out to avoid the cancellation charge!

OTHER METHODS OF GENERATING REVENUE IN CONSULTANCY

For the most part, revenue is generated by fees, which are related to the time spent on a project. A perennial concern in a consultancy practice is the creation of non-time-related income. The reason is simple: if all income is time related, then once you have established your fee rate, there is a theoretical maximum revenue you can get.

If the revenue is to be increased without taking on more employees, the options are to *increase the fee rate* or to *increase the utilization*. My experience of fee rates is that price is rarely the major determinant in the choice of consultant. Other factors being equal, clients will choose the consultancy quoting the lowest fees; the consultancy firms quoting, however, will attempt to ensure that other factors are not equal, but seek to impress through their grasp of the client's problem and the quality of their people. This leads to some tolerance of difference in fee rate; a client would rather pay £50,000 for a consultancy with which he or she was keen to work than £45,000 where the assignment results are expected to be indifferent. So, some increase in fee rate might be possible. There will be a market rate and it may be possible to command a premium; even so, this is unlikely to be much above 10–20 per cent.

The alternative method of increasing revenue is to increase utilization. Again, here there is an upper limit to the number of fee days. Once time has been allowed for annual and statutory holidays, say 30 days per annum, then the number of working days available is down to 230 per person. Out of this, time has to be allowed for:

● sales and marketing;

● product development;

● administration;

● training courses and conferences;

● sickness.

The time spent on each of these will be distributed unevenly across the practice; some consultants will do little other than operating on fees. Others may spend their time primarily on selling (see Figure 4.5 for examples of the budgets for consultants with different roles). The point is that it is difficult to raise utilization to an average of more than 80 per cent without harm in the long term to the practice. Important tasks would be neglected. In practice, too, assignments do not fit neatly together – there are delays to their starting, which means that there is often waiting time for an individual consultant between assignments.

So, the control of fee rate and utilization offers only limited opportunities for increasing revenue. Consultancy managements usually ensure that there are tight controls on utilization; it is monitored frequently (often weekly) and forecasted so that sales efforts can be adjusted accordingly. Fee rates are regularly reviewed, too, so the scope to increase utilization and fee rate is limited in a well-managed practice. If the productivity of existing resources is optimized, how else can revenue be increased?

Payment of a retainer

A retainer represents a step towards non-time-related fees. A simple arrangement is where a consultant reserves a number of days in a period for a client, in exchange for which the client will pay a retainer. If the client does not take the days, then the retainer is still payable. If the client wants more time than the contracted amount, this is subject to negotiation.

Suppose in the ICC case study (Chapter 6), the GM decides that he would like John Smith's services on average for one day per month, not to carry out a specific project, but to provide general advice and counsel. The GM might pay John Smith a retainer for a year of 12 days' fees. There would be rules about John Smith's availability – for example, it would not be in the spirit of the retainer for the GM to take nothing for the first 11 months and insist on 12 days in the twelfth. The rule might therefore be 'up to two days in any one month, and up to six days per quarter; a maximum of 12 days in any one year, additional days to be subject to negotiation'.

Retainers are attractive to a consultancy firm, as they represent a guaranteed fixed base workload. Their usefulness to clients, however, is restricted. Circumstances where they might be applied by clients are:

- with a technical specialist;
- to secure exclusive services (that is, to prevent the client's direct competitors having access to the specialist);
- to secure consultancy services that are not project-based (for example, where a consultant might be used in a temporary, part-time, executive role by a client).

A consultancy practice might also use retainers to secure the services of key subcontractors.

Decoupling price and cost

Professionals typically charge a standard fee rate, irrespective of the value of the work they do, but occasionally the fee can be related to the value of the work – for example: 1) in mergers and acquisition work, a successful transaction is of considerable value to the parties involved – professional advisers may relate their fees to the value of the transaction; 2) in recruitment work, the fees may be related to the emoluments of the appointed candidate.

Sometimes fees will be success related. For example, again in recruitment, at least part of the fee will be conditional on finding a suitable candidate to fill the vacancy. There have also been consultancies that, in their corporate development work, have accepted an equity stake in the company as part payment of their fees.

In theory, consultancies might also receive payment based on the benefits that their assignment has produced. There are arguments against this:

- It can be difficult to produce a satisfactory base case.

- It may influence the consultants to produce recommendations biased towards optimizing their fees rather than the client's business performance.

- Changes may not be the result of the consultancy project (for example, reduced costs can result from a decrease in business activity instead of improved performance).

- Improvements may depend on the performance of client staff as well as the efficiency of the consultancy project.

- There may be a long wait for the consultancy to be paid, as the benefits accrue.

If these points can be satisfactorily addressed, the consultancy charge might be based on the share of the benefits. Some professional organizations, of which consultants are members, may prohibit this basis of fees, and so this should also be checked.

USING SUBCONTRACTORS

Subcontractors are usually paid only for the time they spend on fee earning work. This generates a contribution, being the difference between their daily fee rate and the rate that the client is paying. The related overhead is usually small. Subcontracting has further benefits including:

- It introduces some variability in the cost base. If the volume of sales decreases, you can reduce the amount of subcontract work before you have to consider cutting staff.

- Sub-contractors can be used to bring skills that are not available elsewhere in the consultancy.

The disadvantages of subcontracting are:

- Subcontractors may not be available when you want them, being engaged on projects for other principals.

- Subcontractors are not subject to the same control as full-time employees. This may present difficulties in enforcing a uniformity of approach and standard of quality.

- Subcontractors yield less profit than full-time staff.

The indications are, however, that consultancies are moving the same way as their clients, in that they will use subcontractors increasingly in the future. Indeed, some clients are now insisting that, although overall responsibility for a major project may be given to a large practice, they would expect to see elements of it given to specialist subcontractors and – in some major projects – the work to be conducted by a consortium. This is because it is unlikely that the best consultants or expertise for all elements are in a single practice or, indeed, that the work involved is restricted to consultancy.

NON-TIME-RELATED CHARGES

Consultancy practices can generate income by charging for items related to an assignment, other than the time spent on it. Items that might be charged in such a way include:

- proprietary software;

- use of a proprietary methodology;

- use of psychometric tests and other survey instruments;

- results of research (for example, market research survey);

- organizing conferences or training that the client attends.

For the most part, these represent income from the sale of intellectual property. The consultancy will have invested time and effort in creating the item (or it may have bought a licence from someone who has done so) and is cashing in on this capital.

Sometimes a firm will make a standard charge of a percentage of the fee for 'administration, telephone calls, etc'. This will only approximate to the actual cost, but obviously involves less work than monitoring and costing every administrative expense. The basis of charging expenses should be clear to clients. The danger in making a standard charge is where it is part of the terms of business, which the client has not read properly, so that the first he or she learns about it is when it appears on an invoice from the consultancy.

I have to confess to a personal dislike of this basis of charging for administrative and office expenses; I believe the fee rate should cover all routine costs, with additional charges being made only for exceptional costs on an agreed basis. For example, a consultancy might charge for producing a specialist CD ROM to support a project.

TERMS OF BUSINESS

The commercial aspects of the client relationship are embodied in a practice's terms of business. Unlike terms of reference, which are usually designed for each client project, terms of business are likely to be similar for different projects. Thus far in this chapter, we have considered only the basis of payments made by the client to the consultancy, but there will be other matters that might be routinely included in terms of business, such as:

- intellectual property rights;

- conditions affecting the liability of the consultancy;

- expectations of what the client is to provide;

- other contractual terms, such as how the assignment may be terminated before its completion.

A consultancy practice may have standard terms of business that are included in each proposal, with variations, or optional clauses, which are tailored to a particular contract.

Intellectual property rights

With the growth of the 'knowledge economy', intellectual property rights (IPR) are of increasing importance. This is particularly the case in consultancy, where – presumably – consultants are hired because of their know-how. It is the exercise of this intellectual property that clients are buying, and it would be difficult for a client justifiably to insist that a consultant's know-how became the client's own intellectual property.

IPR becomes a particular issue in matters of specific intellectual property generated on a project, for which a client might reasonably suppose they have paid. This might include, for example:

- product design;

- software development;

- operational processes.

What in theory might happen, for instance, is that a consultancy is paid six months' fees for developing a piece of software for a client A. Another client, B, needs similar software, which would cost six months' fees again, but the consultancy could sell the software developed for Client A. Maybe it might need a month's worth of adjustment, but the consultancy could sell it for five months' fees. Client B would be happy because they have their software at a discount, and the consultancy would be happy because they have five month's revenue for one month's effort. On the other hand, Client A may be less happy at funding this!

Of course, this is a feature of consultancy: consultants acquire learning and experience with clients, which is then deployed to the benefit of later clients. The most that clients can do to protect their interests in this situation is to agree a restriction on future work with direct competitors (see 'Clients' terms of engagement', below). Where intellectual property is developed as a specific product of a project, however, the rights to this should be agreed as part of the terms of business. This, of course, equally applies to the consultancy's intellectual property provided to the client, who may be subject to restrictions on its use.

The liability of the consultancy

In the same way as it is unwise to enter marriage with a divorce settlement in mind, you should never start any consultancy project contemplating its failure. Even so, there are risks associated with all consultancy work, and it is important to have thought through the arrangements if things do not work out as expected.

Although there have been a few court cases in which major practices have been sued, those are exceptional. It is important to have an 'escalation' rather than a 'tripwire' strategy (to use phrases from the Cold War!). In other words, there should be a series of measures in which consultancy and client can engage before resorting to the courts, which is rarely to commercial benefit, although it may apportion blame.

It therefore makes sense to have some form of dispute resolution procedure. In my experience, disputes tend to be about misunderstandings rather than breach of contract, both parties being convinced of rather different things. This reinforces the importance of establishing clear terms of reference at the start, and maintaining effective communications with the client (and documenting agreements) throughout the project.

Expectations of what the client is to provide

Consultancy projects are joint ventures between the consultancy and the client, and it is rare for the client's contribution to be limited simply to funding. Clients' staff will be involved and their time and cooperation will usually be critical to success. In addition, there may be other obligations on what the client is to provide, which may be incorporated within the terms of business, such as:

● office accommodation and facilities;

● secretarial and administrative support;

- logistical help (for example, booking flights, accommodation);

- provision of information.

The detailed nature of these will vary according to the type of work being carried out. For example, in running in-house training courses, a consultancy would want to establish responsibility for:

- making administrative arrangements for participants to attend;

- booking the training venue;

- providing copies of training materials;

- hiring equipment, films, etc.

Other contractual terms

Other contractual terms might include:

- The basis on which fees might be varied. For example, in a time of high inflation, a consultancy might wish to review fee rates during the course of a long project.

- Client confidentiality. This is usually a matter of ethics, and an aspect of each operating consultant's personal contract of engagement. Strictly, it should be superfluous, but clients often take comfort from the confirmation that these arrangements are in place.

- Early termination of contract. There may be circumstances in which a project is rendered no longer necessary, or other occasions in which a client wishes to terminate a contract, or a booking. Cancellation and termination terms should be clear. From the consultancy's side, they will have promised to make the designated consultants available for the required time, and thereby have, usually, turned away alternative pieces of work on which they might be deployed. Cancellation or termination at short notice may mean that it is not possible to find alternative work. Some penalty is usually agreed beforehand; for example, in our training business, we usually insist on full payment if a bespoke training course is cancelled within two weeks of it being due to run. This type of penalty means that clients make cancellations only for serious reasons.

There may be other contractual terms to be placed in your terms of business. Sometimes, however, clients will have their own views of the terms of engagement for consultants.

CLIENTS' TERMS OF ENGAGEMENT

Companies that are frequent users of consultants may themselves have a standard form of consultancy contract they use. This will cover much the same ground as the terms of business of the consultancy practice, but be orientated to the needs of the client rather than the consultancy. I have been subject to these from time to time, and the points of interest in one such are as follows:

- The client reserves the right to ask for replacement of a consultant if in their opinion the performance of the consultant is unsatisfactory.

- Consultants working on the project are subject to approval by the client, approval being based on the consultants' CVs and interview.

- The consultancy should keep records of all activities undertaken on the project, and make them available to the client if so requested.

- The consultancy must show appropriate levels of public liability and professional indemnity insurance.

- There are terms affecting intellectual property rights.

- There are clauses relating to non-solicitation (that is, not poaching the client's employees) and working for the client's direct competitors for a period after the end of the contract.

These topics are ones that relate to all consultancy projects, and therefore can be fairly included as part of the contract. What the consultancy has to do in each case is to decide whether the terms are reasonable. Clients' purchasing departments are likely to have a standard form of contract that they will send to you for agreement. It is then up to you to negotiate with the purchasing department over the details of the clauses in the contract.

8

Operating a consultancy project

A former colleague once explained his view of consultancy thus: 'We are in the business of selling people their dreams', he said. 'Consultants are the dream merchants of business.' This may be the case, but dreams turn into nightmares when consultants promise the unattainable to a client. At best they will have a damaged reputation; in these increasingly litigious times, they may end up being sued.

All that a client buys on purchasing an assignment is a promise; unlike, for example, a car salesperson, a consultant cannot point to the product and say, 'This is what you're going to get.' What you actually get depends on the skills of the consultants delivering the project. In this chapter we consider first the way in which consultancy projects are structured and the skills applying to each phase. Second, we review the demands that consultancy projects make in respect of project management.

THE STRUCTURE OF A CONSULTANCY PROJECT

Irrespective of the level of intervention or the number of phases in a consultancy project, however, you will find that this structure of a project will be similar. The structure of a consultancy project can be broken down into the major stages as shown in Figure 8.1.

Entry

Your first contact with a client may be in selling an assignment or starting an assignment that has already been sold. In either case,

Figure 8.1 The structure of a consultancy project

careful preparation is required and you should aim to make a favourable impact: there is no second chance to make a first impression.

Early in any project it is important to allow time for familiarization. This will be necessary not only for practical matters (such as who's who, office layout etc) but also for understanding the informal rules and climate of the organization. This I call a 'wallow'; it is unstructured data collection, which allows you to soak up the atmosphere and culture of an organization, to learn its 'language' and the myriad of other features that characterize it.

The skills of entry have been covered in Chapter 5 on selling: when consultants meet new clients, they are 'selling' themselves in this role. No further remarks on this are given here.

Contracting

Contracting is about having shared expectations between client and consultant as to what is involved in the project. Selling consultancy is very much a process of product design as well as persuading a client to purchase your services. It is therefore essential to be clear what exactly you are selling, and the specification can be best encompassed in terms of reference dealt with in detail in the sections below.

As soon as contact is made there will be expectations created and commitments made on both sides. These are in addition to the formal agreement set out in the terms of reference. Expectations relate not only to meeting commitments in the terms of reference, but also in how you carry out the project, for example, the apparent priority you attach to the work you are doing for the client. You will also have expectations of the client; these will be reflected largely in the commitment the client shows towards the project.

The sponsor – the member of the client's staff commissioning the project – will, presumably, be committed to it, but you have to consider the commitment of others. Will the project require the cooperation of more senior or more junior staff and, if so, are they committed to the project? Beware of sponsors who are not committed to the project or (at the opposite extreme) who are carrying it out as a personal crusade.

Contracting also covers the practicalities at the start of a project:

- Where will you be working and with what facilities?

- What is the project plan (if this has not been included in the terms of reference)?

- What support will you receive from the client and what form will this take?

- Who will you be dealing with among client staff?

- What have client staff been told about the project – what are their expectations?

Diagnosis

Diagnosis consists of data collection, its analysis and then diagnosis. Paradoxically, you need to consider analysis before deciding what data you need to gather; you have to know what you are going to do with it when you have it. Data gathering is time-consuming and you need to make sure you confine yourself to gathering only that which is necessary and sufficient for your purposes. (See Chapter 6.)

The diagnosis should be drawn from the data collected and consists of conclusions about the nature of the problems being addressed and how they might be resolved. Conclusions answer the question, 'What is the relevance of this data to the areas of concern we are examining?'

Intervention

As a result of the diagnosis, you can then specify the intervention that needs to be made. Because consultants rarely have executive authority within their clients, most often the intervention specified will be in the form of recommendations to be adopted by the client. Whether or not recommendations are accepted is, at least in part, dependent on the influence of the consultant. This topic is discussed later in this chapter.

Closure

When you leave the client, they should have an ongoing capability to maintain the changes and improvements you have introduced as a result of your work. *Transfer* is the process of doing this, and is discussed further at the end of the chapter. It is also important to carry out some sort of *evaluation* of the assignment once it has been completed. This is important not only for quality assurance purposes, but also to ensure that the consultancy practice gets value from the experience of the consultancy team who have carried out the job, for example by capturing:

● the experience of having carried out this work;

● any new operating techniques that have been developed during the project;

● the experience and credibility of working in a particular business sector.

Finally there is *disengagement*. The end of the project may mean the end of this particular piece of work, but there may be extension work, that is, other projects you can carry out to the benefit of the client, or the continuation of the existing project to further levels. Anyhow, the experience of having worked together will have effected a change in the relationship between consultant and client, which should provide a good basis for further work in the future.

CONTRACTING: TERMS OF REFERENCE

If I say to you that I am going to deliver a table to you next Monday, you would have a reasonable idea of what you're going to get. By contrast, if I say to you that I am coming to deliver some consultancy work for you next Monday, you will have far less idea of what you will be getting. Now, there are many kinds of table, so I could perhaps show you a picture of what I am going to deliver. In a similar way, terms of reference are a way of describing what is involved in a consultancy project.

Different consultants will interpret the phrase 'terms of reference' variously. The *Shorter Oxford Dictionary* defines terms of reference as 'the terms which define the scope of an inquiry', and this is a good starting point. Like Humpty Dumpty in *Through the Looking Glass*, however, in this chapter I shall define it to mean what I want it to mean. In my definition, as we shall see, this is enlarged to cover the how and why of the assignment, as well as the deliverables at its conclusion. Whereas terms of reference in this definition relate to the content of a project, terms of business will relate to the commercial context. Terms of business are dealt with in Chapter 7.

Both aspects are usually brought together in a proposal submitted to the client. The proposal is the basis of the contract between consultant and client; it provides the foundation for all that follows within a consultancy project. It lays out the expectations of the client and consultant of each other – an important aspect of managing the client relationship (see Chapter 9).

Terms of reference need to be established clearly for every assignment. Usually they should be written to avoid misunderstandings but, as with any contract, they can be oral as well as written.

Figure 8.2 shows the framework for developing terms of reference. It consists of a statement of:

- the client objectives;

- the assignment objectives;

- the assignment plan.

These three relate together in a hierarchy of objectives: to go up the hierarchy you ask 'Why?'; thus:

Why are we carrying out this plan?
To achieve the assignment objectives.
Why are we aiming at these assignment objectives?
To help the client achieve his or her objectives.

To go down the hierarchy, you ask 'How?', so:

How are the client's objectives to be achieved?
Through achieving the assignment objectives.
How are the assignment objectives to be achieved?
By means of the plan.

```
         ┌─────────────────────────────────────────────────────┐
         │  Client objectives                                  │
Why?     │  Who is the client?                                 │
         │  What does the client want to happen?               │
         └─────────────────────────────────────────────────────┘

                              ⇕

         ┌─────────────────────────────────────────────────────┐
         │  Assignment objectives                              │
         │  Scope : the areas of concern to be addressed       │
What?    │  Outputs : the deliverables to the client           │
         └─────────────────────────────────────────────────────┘

                              ⇕

         ┌─────────────────────────────────────────────────────┐
         │  Assignment plan                                    │
         │  The approach to be used                            │
         │  The programme of work                              │
         │  The resources required (client's as well as        │
How?     │  consultancy's)                                     │
         │  Expected costs and payment schedule                │
         │  Other terms of business                            │
         └─────────────────────────────────────────────────────┘
```

Figure 8.2   Terms of reference

It is worth noting that usually there is only one answer to the question 'Why?', whereas there may be several answers to the question 'How?'. What this means is that the consultancy assignment may be only one of several contributors to the client's objectives. The others, however, may not require consultancy support nor necessarily be in hand. In the following sections we consider each of these three elements comprising terms of reference.

The client objectives

Consultants have to remember that their work is only a means to an end from the client's point of view. A consultant is (rightly) means oriented whereas his or her client is ends oriented. A consultant sees an assignment as a series of tasks, whereas a typical client sees it as a series of deliverables. But you should never lose sight of the context in which you are carrying out the assignment. To this end, you must remain aware who the client is and what the client wants to happen. This can sometimes be difficult when you are engrossed in the minutiae of a complex assignment. (Or, as someone once put it, 'When you're up to your ass in crocodiles, it's hard to remember you came to drain the swamp!')

It is essential to know who the real client is. If we call the person who is dealing with the consultant 'the sponsor' of the assignment, it is important to know if the sponsor is the real client – or is there someone behind the sponsor who is pushing to carry out the project. In the case study on ICC shown in Chapter 6, for example, the sponsor for a consultancy project is the General Manager (GM). What we do not (yet) know is whether John Smith's visit is at the GM's initiative or whether the GM has been pushed into this by a superior. Were the latter true, then this might have a fundamental influence on the GM's attitude to the project. Would he, for example, be a reluctant client? If this were the case, John Smith might find the assignment more difficult – the GM might be unwilling to release resources, make his own time available, and so on. So, what the client wants can be considered at two levels – commercial and personal objectives.

Commercial objectives

These will ultimately relate to:

- improving the performance of the existing business;
- improving its competitive position;
- developing new business.

Obviously the client's objectives for a particular assignment may not be phrased as these; nevertheless, it can be helpful to consultant and client alike to make explicit the causality between the commercial objective as framed and those stated above. This is easy to do in the case of ICC: the client wants to reduce production costs so the company's competitive position and profitability improve.

But what of assignments that are related less directly to commercial objectives – for example, carrying out a job evaluation assignment, helping with an office relocation or delivering a training course? In these cases tracking the client's objectives back to see how they relate to commercial objectives should help fashion the assignment so that it is more helpful to the client.

Personal objectives

These are just as relevant. The assignment sponsor will like the assignment to help him or her to do the job better, to run a better, more efficient department or business, to reflect to his or her credit and so on. Similarly, the sponsor will want to be sure the assignment doesn't go wrong and is not seen as an expensive waste of time. For this latter reason, a key dimension of a consultant's early contact with a sponsor is confidence building.

So, there are general objectives that we can ascribe to the client at the start of an assignment. There may also be specific ones. The consultancy salesperson may have to probe to find these. 'What are the client's unwritten objectives?' should be an item on the checklist of points that the salesperson ought to cover in briefing the operating team. There may be other requirements in terms of the conduct of the assignment:

- The extent to which the sponsor is to be involved in the detail.

- Freedom of access to other parts of the organization (does everything have to be cleared through the sponsor?).

- His or her wish to be involved in helping you in the development of ideas (for example, does the sponsor want to be used as a sounding board, or receive considered views only?).

All this is about setting and understanding expectations, which affects the client relationship. You need to establish a sound modus operandi with the client, which means understanding them personally as well as in their business role.

The assignment objectives

In Figure 8.2, the assignment objectives are defined by scope and outputs: 1) the scope defines the areas of concern that are to be addressed; 2) the outputs are what the client is going to get in respect of each of these areas – the deliverables. Obviously these

Level	Scope	Outputs
1	Sense of organizational malaise	Purposes defined
2	How to achieve the purposes	Main problems that impede their achievement
3	How to resolve defined problems	How they can be best resolved
4	Implementation	Solutions put in place

Figure 8.3 Scope and deliverables for each level of intervention

two together define the amount of work that an assignment might involve. The broader the scope, then the greater amount of work that eventually may be involved. Definition of the deliverables is equally important, particularly because they reflect the depth of analysis that is required to meet them. An in-depth study may need ten times the work of a 'quick and dirty' review.

It is essential that consultancy and client have the same view of these two items. A career-limiting factor in consultancy is to put yourself in a position where you have to do free consultancy because you have overrun your budget. This happens when a client has been promised a deliverable that the consultancy has not achieved within the given budget, or when there has been a mis-understanding over the scope of the assignment. For example, one consultancy agreed to do a study of the manufacturing facilities of a client, believing that there was only one factory site. In fact, there were three; additional resources were therefore required to complete the study.

If you find it difficult to define the scope of the assignment, then you are probably having to deal with a 'messy' problem. Some pre-liminary work may therefore be required in order for the scope to be defined. The assignment therefore has to be broken into phases, the output of each phase defining the scope for the next. This is exemplified in Figure 8.3, which shows the scope and deliverables for the different levels of intervention in a consultancy project. (The idea of 'levels of intervention' was introduced in Chapter 6.)

For example, in the case of ICC (the case study in Chapter 6), we assume that the objective of reducing high production costs has already been agreed, so there is no need to start at level 1. At level 2, John Smith has to verify what the causes of high production costs might be – based on the clues he has found during his initial tour. At the end of the work at this level he should have identified the issues causing high production costs; the level 3 intervention would be to decide how these might be best resolved.

At the start John Smith can only guess what solutions need to be implemented to reduce production costs. The terms of reference, therefore, cannot be comprehensive – he cannot prescribe (other than in the most general terms) what the outcome of the level 3 intervention will be, because the outputs of level 2 set the scope for level 3. He can therefore give firm terms of reference only for his work at level 2. The client may, however, require an estimate of fees for work from identifying the issues through to implementing the solutions. How to deal with this difficulty is dealt with in Chapter 7 under 'What do we tell the client?'

The second element of assignment objectives shown in Figure 8.2 is outputs. Outputs are the deliverables of the assignment. There are two rules for specifying outputs. Firstly, make sure that each item identified within the scope has an output associated with it. An item in the scope with no output raises the question, 'How are you going to address this for the client?' An output unrelated to the scope usually implies the output is related to part of the scope that has not been articulated, in which case the scope should be revised; and that the output is not required (for example, a consultant may produce an assignment report that is primarily for consumption within the consultancy practice instead of being a material means of advancing the performance of the client) in which case you should consider not producing the output.

Secondly, try to define outputs in terms that show how they relate to the client's objectives. 'So what?' analysis can be helpful here – ask 'So what?' of each output to see whether it relates to the client objective. (This is particularly useful when tempted to produce outputs consisting only of data feedback.)

Figure 8.4 shows the scope and outputs for ICC for interventions at level 2 and 3.

At the start of his assignment, John Smith has accepted the purpose that production costs have to be reduced, but can only guess what areas need to be tackled to reduce them. At the end of the

Level	Scope	Outputs
2	How can production costs be reduced?	The major issues resulting in high product costs identified
3	Wastage and rework rates	Report on how to reduce them
	Machine downtime	Recommend improved maintenance schedule
	Customer expectations of quality	Recommended changes to product specifications
	Suppliers' prices	Recommendations on improved purchasing policies and procedures

Figure 8.4 Assignment objectives

level 2 intervention, therefore, his output is a more focused view of the areas that might be investigated in more detail.

Suppose at the end of this intervention he has identified the items shown in Figure 8.4 as the problems causing high production costs. At the next level of intervention (level 3) the deliverables could be the reports and recommendations shown in the figure. If he were then to help the client with a level 4 intervention, he would support the implementation of his recommendations.

I used to be worried that the output that a consultant produces so often consists of reports and recommendations – hardly a direct intervention into the client environment. But given that a consultant rarely has executive authority within a client's firm, outputs for action or a decision are usually expressed in terms of recommendations. Of course, the skill of the consultant lies in not only making the recommendations, but also in getting them accepted. (See later in this chapter.)

Although consultants can forecast outputs (that is, immediate deliverables), they should be more conservative when forecasting outcomes or results. If the consultancy has total control of the factors influencing outcomes, then they can be more confident of predicting what the results of an assignment might be. Usually, however, a consultancy assignment is a joint activity between consultant and client, and so the results will depend on the cooperation and skill of the client staff, and the vagaries of the business environment. For these reasons, it is unusual for a consultancy to be able to guarantee the results of an assignment in terms of – say – decreased costs or increased performance. If it were rash enough to do so, and the expected results were not achieved, the client might reasonably claim some sort of redress.

What is most helpful under these circumstances is for the consultancy to indicate conditionally what the outcomes might be. 'Given the cooperation of your staff, we would expect costs to be reduced by 5–10 per cent.' Or, 'Based on our experience elsewhere, we would expect this programme to increase the department's performance by at least 5 per cent.' These statements do not guarantee the results will be achieved; even so, some consultancies would prefer to use phrasing that is more non-committal. They may also have a disclaimer in their terms of business such as that reproduced below:

Forecasts, etc by the Consultant

The time taken to complete the work and the measure of its success depend in part on factors outside the control of the Consultant. These include the degree of cooperation given by the Client's staff and promptness in agreeing and implementing recommendations. Any forecast or estimate made by the consultant of the time required for the assignment and the results attainable is given in good faith having regard to the information made available by the Client and represents the Consultant's interpretations of the Client's instructions. Any such estimates and any confirmation or variation of them in subsequent reports and correspondence shall not be deemed in any circumstances to be undertakings, warranties or contractual conditions. (*Source*: Institute of Management Consultancy)

Assignment plan

The items shown in the box 'Assignment plan' in Figure 8.2 can themselves be related in a hierarchy of objectives thus:

How are we going to implement this approach?
By carrying out this programme of work.
How are we going to carry out this programme of work?
By utilizing these resources.

The hierarchy can again be ascended by asking the question 'Why?'

Resources may be drawn from both client and consultant. It is essential that the client recognizes the resources they must provide, both in the conduct of the assignment and its management (see below). And, of course, the consultancy will be providing resources for a price. This price, with the other aspects relating to the commercial context of the business, will be embodied in the terms of business – see Chapter 7.

Deciding the method of approach

The approach to be used relies on an appraisal of how the consultancy team and client are respectively to contribute to the achievement of the assignment objectives. From this appraisal all the work on the assignment is predicated. As a consultant, you must be clear about what you are bringing to the party. This will determine what your role is, and it has to be complementary to that of the client. At one extreme you can be highly interventionist and take much of the project onto your own shoulders. At the other extreme, the role of the consultant is facilitative, enabling the clients to address the problem for themselves. Between these two extremes is a spectrum of consultancy roles, and you must decide which is appropriate.

In some cases, the client hands over a project to the consultant and there is no further contact until the work is complete. Such assignments are often research oriented. For example, a client might ask a consultant to identify the size of market and buying criteria for a product in Zambia. The consultant would carry out the research and then report to the client.

For the most part, however, assignments are cooperative efforts between consultant and client. Even in a research oriented assignment a consultant will probably have some reviews with the client between beginning and end. For instance, in the ICC case study, the GM will probably arrange for John Smith to have access to records, people, equipment and other resources, to enable him to diagnose the key problems (the level 2 intervention). John Smith will engage in data collection and report back with his conclusions.

In the next phase, he will need to decide how the problems he has identified should be addressed, which may entail the active involvement of some of ICC's staff. They might, for example, engage in data collection, contribute their ideas, or plan operational improvements. Different modes of client and consultant working together can therefore be involved even in a simple assignment.

The next consideration in deciding the method of approach concerns the perception of the nature of the predicament. A client may see the issues to be dealt with in more simple terms than the consultant and would therefore not be in favour of an approach that treated it as complicated. In the example of ICC, the GM might see the problems of production cost being entirely due to poor quality production. He may even have employed John Smith to come up with the conclusion that high production costs are entirely the result of poor equipment performance, and to use this as a lever for getting capital investment out of his head office.

No consultant will retain the goodwill of a client by speaking against the client's favourite ideas on day one. Remember the dictum, 'Sell the client what they need in terms of what they want'; the consultant has to educate the client into the true nature of the issues that have to be addressed. The client's perception of these may therefore develop throughout the course of an assignment. This does not mean active opposition. If you set up an 'either/or' situation (either your view prevails, or mine) then you will lose – certainly in the long term. You should establish a 'both/and' view, that is, 'We will investigate both your ideas and others, which from the evidence and our experience, we believe will help to achieve your objective.' The client can be brought round to the consultant's view – if appropriate – later in the project.

A further point you must consider when deciding the method of approach occurs when a client is embarking on a project that represents a significant change to the business. You need to know whether the problem solving processes available within the client's organization are appropriate for dealing with this problem. For example, there are some organizations in which most of the transactions are oral and face to face – little is written down. One such was a business in which the founder and owner was a 'dealer' – an entrepreneur who had built the business on his skills in striking good deals. The method of problem solving in the business derived from this process: problems were resolved at a round table discussion culminating with a 'deal' – who was going to do what. While this approach was effective for many operational problems in the business, it was less effective in coping with more complex problems of a strategic nature. The consultant had to educate the client in other methods of problem solving, by setting up a working party to study the issues and helping the client use a multi-stage approach to dealing with them.

In summary, therefore, in deciding the method of approach, the consultant has to consider the following:

- What are the skills and resources consultant and client can respectively bring to solving this problem?

- What is the client's expectation of the consultant's role and how appropriate is this?

- What is the client's view of the problem (and how does it differ from that of the consultant)?

- What is the nature of the predominant problem solving procedures within the client's firm?

- What are the skills and resources the client can bring to solving this problem?

Programme of work

Once the method of approach has been established, the programme of work explains what is going to happen and when. This is in effect the assignment plan. Sometimes clients find it difficult to visualize how the consultancy will accomplish the assignment objectives. The assignment plan helps by showing how the transition is to be made from the present situation to the new one. It is therefore a good way of building a client's confidence in the project.

Project planning

There is often a reluctance to plan, but planning is vital if projects are to be delivered on time, good client relationships are to be preserved and budgeted time and resources are not to be exceeded. One reason for this reluctance is that planning can be difficult in complex situations, or at the start of a project when there are a lot of unknowns. In such circumstances, it is sensible to break a project into a number of stages, each dependent on the findings of the former. The use of explicit planning assumptions can also be helpful in dealing with this. As the project progresses, the validity of these assumptions can be tested and the plan modified in the light of any revised assumptions.

Project planning should start during the bidding process for a project, when it will be necessary to estimate the time and other resources required to carry out the project. The elements of a project plan will consist of:

- a breakdown of the deliverables to be produced by the project, derived from the project objectives;

- a breakdown of the project into the tasks or work packages required to produce these deliverables;

- a logic diagram showing the sequence and dependencies of these tasks;

- the resources required for each task.

When the start date for the project has been confirmed, two other elements have to be added:

- a list of the specific individuals (from whatever source) who will work on the project, with exact details of their availability both in terms of the number of hours a week they will be working, and the dates when they will be unavailable;

- a timetable showing when each activity will be done, and who will do it.

If the project consists of a number of phases, a plan will need to be prepared for each phase. In addition to other elements involved, every project plan should include:

- *Milestones* at which the progress of a project can be assessed.

- *Formal progress reviews* attended by the project manager, the account manager and the client. (Informal progress reviews may take place more frequently.) These should coincide at least with milestones, and may be held more frequently.

- *Schedule of deliverables*. When deliverables (for example, reports) are to be produced for the client.

- *Invoicing schedule*. When the client is to be invoiced for the project.

With projects of any complexity (involving a number of consultants), time should be allowed in the project plan for project administration, such as briefing and review meetings with consultants.

Resources required

The programme of work will specify the tasks needed to be carried out by the consultant team, and hence the resources the consultancy has to provide. The fees that are charged to the client will be related to the cost of the assignment. This in turn will be based on an estimate of the time required from each consultant multiplied by his or her fee rate. The accuracy of the estimate of the time required is thus central to the profitability (or otherwise) of a consultancy project. If there are a number of people engaged in a project, a 'Time and responsibilities schedule' should be issued on a regular basis showing:

● the tasks to be accomplished;

● who is responsible for each task;

● the resources (time, other) to be devoted to the task;

● when the task has to be completed.

A schedule may cover only those tasks in the immediate future; further schedules can be issued as a project progresses.

It is worth making explicit the resources you will need from a client to carry out an assignment. Sometimes these are clear – for example, when a member of client staff is to be assigned to the project team – but there are other workload implications for a client embarking on a consultancy assignment. For example, the client resources a consultant might need are accommodation, access to a telephone, use of secretarial support (for example, for fixing meetings) and other office services. The consultant will also need time from the sponsor to carry out progress reviews. There may be more active involvement of client staff – responding to interviews and questionnaires, or communicating aspects of the project to staff within the organization.

How the project is to be managed

All projects require some input from clients, if only to act as a reporting link. More is usually required, for example, to take decisions. Not all clients are accustomed to using consultants and it may be necessary to advise a client on the appropriate organization to manage the project internally. A question that consultant and client need to debate is, 'Can this project be managed within the ordinary processes of management, or does it require extraordinary arrangements for its management?' In the latter case (which happens more often than not) special arrangements need to be made.

Managerial and other resources required from a client should be made clear at a project's inception. The consultant should also comment on the organization structure that the client should establish for dealing with the project. The simplest structure applies when a consultant reports simply to the sponsor of the project. At the other extreme is a major project being run by an organization, in which the consultancy firm is making a subcontractor's contribution within an established organization structure.

Between these two extremes lies the project steering group. This can consist of the consultancy project manager and the client sponsor, plus other members. The selection of other members is significant. If senior members of departments affected by the project are co-opted onto the steering committee, they should provide helpful counsel, and their participation should help to get better acceptance of any changes proposed. A steering committee also gets a broader exposure for the consultancy firm, and reduces its vulnerability to reliance on a single sponsor. Obviously there are many variations on this theme such as a project steering group that reports to a more senior committee, or subgroups that are responsible for particular aspects of the project.

Consultancy practices will have had more experience of dealing with consultancy projects than their clients, and therefore should always consider what is the most appropriate form of client organization. In some circumstances this may mean challenging the project organization that the client may have in place already.

DIAGNOSIS: MANAGING CONSULTANCY PROJECTS

Having set up the consultancy project, much of the work then involves problem solving and data collection – topics already covered in Chapter 6. In this section we consider how the project itself is to be managed during its course.

Consultancy work is mostly project-based so all consultants have to have skills in project management. At one end of the project spectrum is the project of perhaps only a few days done by a single consultant. At the other is the major project of a year or more involving a large team of consultants, subcontractors and so on. All demand skills of project management.

The effectiveness with which a project is executed will depend in large measure on the quality of project management. It is not the purpose of this text to provide a comprehensive treatise on project management; there are several standard methodologies available, some of which are used by consultancy practices. Whether or not you are using a standard project management system, however, from the point of view of managing the practice, you need to be assured that project management is being carried out to an appropriate standard of performance.

We have already considered the project plan under terms of reference above. The plan provides a forecast of activity and resources. Without a plan, it is impossible to monitor how things are going and thereby to take corrective action when required.

Principles of project planning and control

I find the metaphor of a journey a useful one to gain an insight into the key components of a project. In planning a journey you have to know where you are going and when you need to be there. You must decide what route you are to take, which means that you need to know where you're starting from and whether there are any limitations on the route you can take. (For example, is the aim to take the fastest route, the prettiest route, or the most economical? Do you need to make a detour to pick some people up on the way?) You will need to make sure that you have the right resources for your trip. (Are you going by car or another form of transport? Will you need to take food?)

Suppose that you are to travel from London to Bristol by road, to arrive in Bristol at a specific time. If you are to be able to control the implementation of your plan, you need to monitor how you are doing; you need to have 'milestones', so that at predetermined points on your route, say Reading and Swindon, you can judge whether you are ahead or behind schedule, and act appropriately. You will also need to be able to tell when you have arrived in Bristol.

On your journey you may have to change your plans because a road might be closed, or there is a severe traffic jam. Indeed, there may be a radio report that causes you to decide to change your destination; you are going to Bristol for a holiday, but reports of bad weather make you decide to go to Exeter instead. Plans may therefore need to change to take account of changed circumstances.

From the metaphor of a journey, you can infer the important features of project planning and control for a consultant:

1. You have to know the purpose of the assignment and why the client wants it done. The deliverables from the project and the timing of their delivery must be defined, stated and agreed.

2. You need to decide what steps are involved in achieving the assignment objectives, and what, if any, subsidiary objectives might affect this plan.

3. You need to ensure you have the resources required.

4. If you are to be able to control the project, you need to programme in some milestones, that is, points during the project at which you can judge progress. It is too late to wait until the end to ask, 'Did we make it?'

5. No business stands still; during the course of an assignment of any duration a business will have moved on. It is therefore probable that the detailed requirements of the assignment will also change.

Other aspects of this metaphor are also helpful; for example, to go on a journey you have to leave your point of departure. Sometimes client staff don't want to leave the past behind, but there will be no progress unless they do.

Project control

Project control is the process of monitoring actual activity and events against those projected in the project plan. It follows that if the plan is poor, control will be more difficult – control can be only as good as the plan itself. The project manager should maintain records of:

- dates when tasks and phases have been completed;

- dates when deliverables have been made to the client;

- the consumption of time and fees and other resources against budget;

- any other aspects relating to the management of the quality of the project.

If several consultants are involved in a project, the project manager must gather this information regularly from each member of the project team.

It is often useful for the project manager (and consultants in the project team) to keep a 'project diary' – a notebook in which all information relating to the project can be kept. This includes notes of telephone calls, meetings, key decisions and so on. A project diary is particularly necessary when working on projects that are deemed risky. The commercial aspects of risk are dealt with in Chapter 7; there are also operating risks, which occur in the following situations:

- where the project is complex, or depends on innovative techniques;

- where a major section of the client staff is antagonistic to the project;

- where the client is unreliable, for example, in not providing resources as promised;

- where the project is politically sensitive;

- where the consultancy resources are likely to be overstretched;

- where the terms of reference are ill-defined, or likely to change during the project.

The project manager should exercise control through progress reviews. A progress review should be held at each milestone, or more frequently, as set out in the plan. The progress review should cover:

- progress: achievements to date and use of resources, compared with budget;

- problems, actual or anticipated;

- plans, including short-term action, addressing problems, and rescheduling tasks.

This may be summarized in a progress report, which might in addition comment on:

- key meetings held with clients;

- opportunities for further work following on from the project.

The project manager should conclude the report with an overall appraisal of project progress and the state of the client relationship.

During the course of a project, circumstances change and more information becomes available, and so plans made at the start of a project may no longer be appropriate. Replanning should therefore be regarded as the rule, not the exception with projects extending more than several months. Project plans should be amended accordingly. Replanning may influence two important factors: 1) the scheduling of resources and 2) the ability to honour commitments made to clients.

Managing expectations is an important component of maintaining a good client relationship (see Chapter 9). If replanning is necessary, consider what the impact of this will be on the client, and how they should be best kept informed.

Keeping the client informed

Client expectations have to be carefully managed, and this must be done through regular contacts with the client. Progress reviews with the client should form part of the project plan. It is particularly important to make sure that the client is kept well informed during the early stages of a project. This is the period when the client may feel more insecure if nothing is heard; frequent reassurance that all is going to plan will build the confidence of the client. The policy with clients should be 'No surprises'.

It is a feature of consultancy projects that things occasionally go wrong, perhaps through unfortunate circumstances, accident, failure of a consultant or client, or simply because individuals do not get on. These situations can be managed and rectified only if they are recognized and dealt with before they become crises. Very often the consultant can handle them alone; on other occasions more help may be required. This can be provided only if the consultant says that help is needed. Similarly, client confidence is bolstered by achievements, and so these should be publicized to the client whenever appropriate.

Changing terms of reference

When engaged in the detail of a project, it is easy to lose sight of the project objectives, let alone why the client commissioned it. The terms of reference should be referred to frequently, to ensure the project keeps on track.

It is not unusual for terms of reference to change during a project. This may be because circumstances have changed, or because new information has become available, which means that the scope or outputs of the assignment should change.

It is important that the same rigour of thinking goes into revised terms of reference as in the original. Again, it is essential that client and consultant have expectations in common. Consequently, it is sensible to secure the client's agreement and to document any changes. This is particularly important if the original terms of reference are written. Although changes might be orally agreed, a change of job incumbent or a deterioration in the client relationship may require there to be evidence of the agreed change. In such circumstances, therefore:

1. The implications of the change on the existing project should be assessed.

2. The change and its implications should be discussed and agreed with the client.

3. The change should be documented, in particular noting changes in deliverables, timescales and fees.

As mentioned above, clients' circumstances change over time, so on longer projects changing terms of reference should not be regarded as unusual.

INTERVENTION

The culmination of a consultancy project is the intervention stage of the consultant's interaction with the client, particularly in respect of getting recommendations accepted. By recommendations I mean not only substantive advice from the consultant as an expert, but also suggestions about processes in which a client might engage, with the consultant in a supporting role. Implementation of a consultant's recommendations is often in two parts: 1) the translation of recommendations into decisions, which is done at an executive level in an organization and 2) the translation of recommendations (or decisions) into action, which may be done at more junior levels. Intervention is discussed in these two respects later in this chapter, but first, we need to consider how to formulate high-quality recommendations.

Consultants are occasionally likened to giant birds that fly into an organization, excrete a fat report, and then fly off again. Obviously there will be occasions when this is just what is wanted. But if the intention is to do something more, failure may be the result of poor recommendations.

Formulating high-quality recommendations

So, what makes for high-quality recommendations? There are three criteria to be considered:

● technical adequacy – will they work?

● acceptability to the client;

● the capacity of the client to implement them – their do-ability.

Technical adequacy

This criterion is the most familiar and straightforward: will the recommendations help the client to address the assignment objectives satisfactorily? Given that the purpose of a consultancy assignment is to do just this, then I hope that the answer is 'Yes'. If in doubt, refer to the terms of reference!

Every assignment should have a spice of originality to the recommendations. No two clients are identical, and so it is unlikely that identical recommendations will be suitable. And, if they are, it should be because alternatives have been considered and abandoned.

Most consultants come to the profession having their roots in some sort of specialized knowledge. So, for example, a marketing consultant will probably have both some formal, academic grounding in the topic as well as previous experience, perhaps, in an executive role in marketing. He or she will therefore, as a subject matter expert, arrive at recommendations that will be excellent for the client, but these may need to be compromised in order to meet the remaining criteria – acceptability and do-ability.

Acceptability

A consultant will often need to work hard to get his or her recommendations accepted and implemented by a client. But if a recommendation is profoundly unacceptable – not in the interests of the client or of influential members of client staff – then compromise is necessary. For example, a consultancy team advising on organizational issues took the view that the newly appointed Chief Executive was the wrong person to lead a particular client forward. The ideal recommendation was to replace him, but soundings showed there was insufficient support for this among the other directors. The compromise was to strengthen the executive team so that the Chief Executive would have adequate support in carrying out the tasks in the areas in which he was weakest.

Acceptability will also be conditional on the culture and values of the organization. For instance, there may be 'rules' about how change may be introduced; for instance, 'no redundancies'.

So, you can define a 'state of readiness' of a client for recommendations of different kinds. The reality, however, is that this is rarely dispersed uniformly across the organization. Frequently, there are differences at various levels of management; top management, for example, embraces structural change as a means of performance development, while middle management – who perhaps see the disadvantages more clearly – are usually more reserved.

Do-ability

The history of foreign aid to less developed countries abounds in stories of well-meaning donations of sophisticated equipment that cannot be repaired when it breaks down, because of a lack of spare parts, or there is no infrastructure to distribute them, or insufficient skill to fit them properly. From this difficulty arose the notion of intermediate technology – not the most advanced, but that which a recipient country can sustain.

Similar considerations apply to clients; their organizations may be unable to sustain the 'best' technical solution. The consultant may install it, and it works well for a while, but at the first sign of difficulty the new system breaks down irretrievably as far as the client is concerned. So again compromise may be necessary.

Points for consideration are:

- Has the client got the necessary resources – managerial, financial – to sustain this solution?

- Has the client got the skills (technical, systems) to support this solution?

- Is this solution consistent with the client's culture and style of management? Solutions that require a fundamental change in client culture or behaviour are more susceptible to failure.

Translating recommendations into decisions

Having got high-quality recommendations adopted by executives, will they be translated into decisions? Whether they are accepted depends on two factors: 1) the consultant's influence, which will affect the weight that the client attaches to what the consultant says; 2) the attractiveness (or otherwise) of the specific recommendations. If a consultant's view carries little weight, then it will be difficult for him or her to get recommendations accepted irrespective of how sound they are.

This is not only about how to present recommendations to best effect. Recommendations are like tender young plants; the ground has to be prepared carefully beforehand if they are to flourish. Similarly, the conduct of the assignment must provide a basis for the warm reception of the recommendations.

The nature of a consultant's influence

By definition, consultants have no legitimate executive authority within the client organization. Sometimes they may have delegated authority; members of client staff may be assigned to work under their direction on a consultancy project, but this authority will be within strict confines. For the most part, however, a consultant can only influence rather than mandate the decision-making processes within a client.

So, what power does the consultant have? It is the consultant's expertise – knowledge, skill, experience, know-how – that gains him or her admission into a client organization. If you do not have expertise, then you cannot act as an expert. Once inside an organization, another type of power also comes into play – connection power. The consultant will often have been appointed by executives more senior than the client staff with whom the consultant is working on a day to day basis. Connection power gives a power of sanction – if junior staff are not cooperative, then the consultant can use connections at a senior level to make things happen. Because of the connection with key people, the consultant may come into possession of information about situations, plans and so on, which is not generally known. This can help in planning how to exert influence. Moreover, client staff may pay more heed to consultants if they believe that they are privy to, and have an influence over, their future careers.

It is the perception of power that leads to influence; for example, irrespective of how skilled you are, if you are not credited with any expertise, you will have no expert power. You therefore need to make careful efforts to develop your influence by using your expertise for cultivating connections within the client and using these connections to exercise influence.

Your behaviour will also determine the degree of influence you have. Consider:

- *How do you see yourself?* People will initially take you at your own valuation. If you have a low opinion of yourself, your abilities, or your standing with the client, this will come across. Consultants should not be arrogant, but neither are they supplicants.

- *What impression do you make?* From day one of their career, consultants are taught that first impressions count. It is a point so well known that it may not seem worthwhile repeating, yet it still creates difficulties. So, remember that your appearance, what you say, and how you comport yourself, will affect the impression that you make. And be natural –

clients are offended if you try to pretend to be something that you're not.

- *How do you and your colleagues treat one another?* If you treat one another with disdain, what is the client to make of this? For example, there was a director of a consultancy who was introducing a young consultant to a client. During the meeting, the director peremptorily asked his colleague to fetch his briefcase from his car. Although the director was undoubtedly the senior, he had undermined the standing of his junior colleague with that client from the start.

Optimizing expert power

For the most part, a consultant starts with a fund of expert power – an expectation that he or she is expert in their area of specialization. What the consultant says or does enhances or diminishes this. The wrong appearance or asking foolish questions, revealing a lack of knowledge will undermine the perception of the consultant's expertise. The perception of expert power will derive not only from what the consultant says and does, but also from, firstly, the label of 'consultant'. Being labelled a consultant is not always a passport to friendly acceptance by client staff. Negative feelings can arise from consultancy projects in the past that have led to painful change, previous experience of poor quality consultancy service or dislike of the consultant's role, fee rate, etc. Nevertheless, the label of consultant should create an expectation of having at least some expertise.

Secondly, the 'source effect' of the consultant's firm. 'Source effect' is the equivalent of the branding of the consultancy firm; it derives from its reputation. If the consultant works for a practice that is known to the client, he or she will take on some of the attributes of that consultancy. (By analogy, for example, if you go as a patient into a hospital, you assume that the person called 'doctor' knows about medicine!)

Developing expert power comes by displaying technical expertise. This must be complemented by understanding. Airing technical knowledge is unlikely to impress a client; applying technical knowledge to a client's problems in a helpful way, and explaining this in terms the client understands will help to enhance your influence.

Optimizing connection power

Connection power derives from contact with important or influential members of client staff, so it is important therefore that a consultant preserves connections with them. For example, the mechanism of a steering committee can be used in project management to maintain contacts with senior people, and to escalate the level of contact within an organization.

Maintaining appropriate contacts within the client organization is, in effect, networking – a concept that we have already met in connection with selling. In this instance the consultant is trying to 'sell' him- or herself within the client organization. To this end, you should seek to establish and maintain a variety of links within the client organization. Every interaction with the client will affect how you are perceived. While preparing for meetings, interviews, presentations or any other interaction, therefore, you must consider not only the business of the meeting, but also how it might be used to develop your influence in the client. For example, suppose that at the start of an assignment you have to collect information from each director on the client's board. This provides an excellent opportunity for the consultant to form relationships with the key executives in the client organization. The risk is that the consultant sees this as solely data collection, thereby missing this opportunity.

Exercising influence

So far we have been considering the nature of a consultant's influence – the accretion of expert and connection power, so that when he or she speaks, what is said commands at least some attention. Next, we need to consider the exercise of this influence, so as to get adoption of particular recommendations. Getting recommendations adopted starts long before their presentation, and entails managing informal as well as formal communications with the client.

Informal communications

All interactions with a client are interventions into the client environment, and have to be managed as such. For example, in an interview programme, the consultant might start the process of change by asking a single question. For example, 'Has the company ever considered moving to a lower cost location?' might prompt this consideration if none had previously been given.

It is often useful to get reaction to ideas well before presenting them, during progress reviews and other meetings or encounters with key executives. You can trail them without commitment: 'One of the suggestions that has been made is... ', or, 'We came across this idea at another client's... '. Discussing the way your thinking is going can also elicit useful information that can help you in reformulating or refining recommendations.

Formal communications

Formal communications will consist of face to face presentations and meetings, and reports and other written communications. This book does not cover the details of how to prepare and deliver presentations to a high standard (see Markham, 2003, for details on these).

The choice of who to communicate to is important. Key influencers within the organization are an obvious choice, but remember, firstly, you may not have direct access to them; you may therefore need to deal (at least initially) with connectors who act as gatekeepers to them. Secondly, the power to say 'No' is widely distributed throughout an organization. Although someone may not be able to make something happen, they may be able to stop it. So remember you will need to convince those who can stop a proposal as well as those who can make it happen.

Matching communication style with the decision-making style of the organization

The style with which an organization takes decisions is on a spectrum from action oriented to reflective. Organizations with an action oriented style will like face to face communications. They will appreciate being presented with the key points and will aim to sort out what has to be done at a single meeting. By contrast, those organizations with a reflective style will prefer to receive a paper on a topic, which is then discussed at a committee meeting.

Working with each has its pros and cons. The action oriented likes to get things done quickly. The disadvantage is that this does not work when dealing with complex problems. For example, one professional services firm was reviewing how it could best develop its business in the midst of a recession. The approach among partners was for each to assert what the solution was and seek to persuade their colleagues of it. This did not allow any effort to be put into thinking about what the nature of the problem was, and so the action taken was not particularly effective.

The reflective style does allow debate about the nature of the problem, but it can also be frustrating for an action oriented organization. For example, a financial services group was considering restructuring its bonus plan, which had profound implications for their (very strong) culture. The consultant sought to explore the issues by presenting a series of papers to a steering committee. The steering committee wanted more speedy action, and so became increasingly frustrated, until the work reached the implementation stage. Here, the consultant had failed to match the required style; a more action oriented approach was required.

This difference of style applies to individuals, too, who can be action oriented, or reflective, or somewhere between the two. The consultant needs to suit the manner of communication to the style. Papers will be read only cursorily by the action oriented, while a reflective manager will not like to make a decision of any moment without a paper being presented on the topic first.

One of a consultant's functions is educative, leaving clients better able to deal with the matters of concern addressed on the assignment (see 'Transfer' later in this chapter). The consultant may need to educate the client in different methods of decision making, so that the issues may be dealt with effectively. In doing so, you have to be careful not to be so countercultural as to be rejected.

Translating recommendations into action

The challenges for a consultant in turning recommendations into action are:

- getting recommendations accepted by those affected and gaining their commitment;

- managing the change process;

- ensuring that the client has an ongoing capability to support the change after implementation, so that transfer takes place.

Gaining commitment

Although in theory it is possible to demand compliance with a change, positive commitment from those affected will yield better results. The following will help to build commitment:

- *Changes should be owned and supported by the client organization.* Any change should be seen as an initiative being taken by the client organization rather than being identified with the consultants. Active and visible support from top management is required. Giving the project a name can also help (for example, a TQM (total quality management) project might be entitled 'Project Gold'). This conclusion is supported by research, which shows that the majority of change programmes fail to deliver the results that were anticipated. The successful ones have one dominant feature: the active commitment and involvement of top management.

- *Participation leads to commitment.* People will become more committed if they are kept informed and participate in decisions. The sooner this starts, the better. It may not be possible to involve everybody from the start (for example, before a decision has been made to proceed), but thereafter involvement should be more than is usual. For example, although junior members of staff may not decide where their office is to be located, they might have a say in the layout and decor of where they work.

  More time and resources need to be allowed for communication during a change – existing communication arrangements may not be adequate by themselves. Similarly, there may need to be more participation in decision making. A useful technique here is 'reservations in the right to decide'. Rather than delegating specific decisions to those affected by the change, define those that they should not make, and then leave the remaining decisions to them.

- *Honour resistance.* Resistance is the opposite of commitment, and dealing with it usually means overcoming it. Richard Beckhard, however, talks of 'honouring resistance' (Beckhard, 1989). This attaches a value to those who resist by assuming that they do so for what to them are sound reasons. These reasons could be germane to the success of the project, and ignoring them would be foolish.

There will be some people, however, who cannot make the change and therefore resist it irrationally and may eventually have to transfer jobs or leave the organization if the change is to be implemented successfully.

Managing the change process

Implementing change is a process, and it is a process that has to be managed. The previous section on gaining commitment implied that change often involves new ways of communicating and taking decisions. Key points in managing a change process are:

1. *Allow sufficient resources for carrying out the change.* Not only does the substance of change take time, but so too does the process. There is rarely enough organizational slack to enable people to undertake a major change while continuing with their existing level of work. Some reallocation of tasks to allow those involved the time to carry out the change is necessary, as well as support from outside consultants.

2. *Launch the change.* Running some sort of event to mark the start of the change process can raise its profile and start the unfreezing process. A training course, workshop, 'kick-off' meeting or similar event can be used.

3. *Work with key people.* There will be key people on whom you should devote more time than the rest. You should identify who can make a major difference to the success or failure of the project (not everybody will) and spend a disproportionately large amount of time with them.

4. *Nurse the change during the early stages.* There are bound to be teething problems with any change, and so more support is required during the early stages when people are learning the

new ways. When trying anything new, performance falls (for example, when a baby starts to walk, it makes less progress than when it crawled). People will need reassurance that this is to be expected, and does not mean that the change has failed.

5. *Give feedback and celebrate success.* People need to know how they are doing; feedback is therefore particularly important during the change process. Celebrating major milestones marks the successful progress of change.

6. *Make sure that psychological and material rewards do not act as a barrier to change.* People will be inhibited from changing if a bonus scheme, or the basis of performance appraisal, career progression, or simply what managers praise, is oriented to the old arrangements. You should therefore make sure that rewards are modified to be consistent with changed circumstances.

CLOSURE

Transfer

A key aspect of closure is transfer.

Transfer is the process of making sure the client has an ongoing capability to support the change after the consultant has gone. Methods of effecting transfer include:

- training;
- writing manuals and programmes;
- establishing systems and procedures.

Key points are, firstly that *transfer is part of the project.* If consultant and other resources are not contracted for transfer, it won't happen. Transfer should be included, where appropriate, in the terms of reference and provisions should be made in the project costing for carrying it out. Secondly, *transfer should include follow-up.* Follow-up visits by the consultant can be used to ensure that transfer has been successful, and can be used to deal with any problems that might have cropped up. A further advantage of follow-up is to consultants – it gives them a further right of entry to a client organization, and therefore provides a commercial opportunity.

Evaluation

Finally, there needs to be some sort of review of the project. At a superficial level, evaluation is simply assessing the degree to which the client was satisfied; but on a project of any significant size, you should carry out a case review, which identifies the key learnings arising from the project and records these on the practice's knowledge management system. Case review can also be done jointly with the client – not only leading to richer results but in a growth in the relationship.

9

Managing client relationships

The Managing Director of a small family company was recounting his experiences with consultants over the previous 10 years. 'My father started the business and, like many entrepreneurs, was very resistant to advice. It was only when we were approaching bankruptcy that we got in our first consultant – who saved us.

'Since then, our experience has been mixed. One consultant produced a report on meeting BS 5750, which was four times as thick as necessary. He simply duplicated what he'd done for his last client; it was a disaster. The next – an energy consultant – didn't tell us anything we didn't know already and failed to tell us some things we already knew.

'We had some craft training done by an outsider; that went well. We also got a consultant in to help us introduce payment by cheque for all staff. Not only did he do this, but he also gave us a valuable report on our industrial relations.

'Later, we had a consultant from a highly reputable firm to advise us on our marketing. We had some specific questions to which we particularly wanted answers. The consultant didn't bother answering our questions. The only impact he had on our business was one of creating annoyance.'

It takes so much effort to win a client, but very little to lose them. Selling has often been likened to courtship; but after the client has been won, the eagerly courted girlfriend can become a neglected wife, who complains, 'You never bring me flowers any more.' In one instance, a consultant promised a proposal to a new director of a long-standing client. Owing to pressure of other work, the consultant

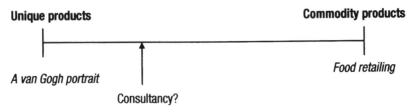

Figure 9.1 A spectrum of products and services

forgot his promise and failed to submit the proposal (a situation unique in my experience!). The director was so incensed that he persuaded his colleagues not to use the consultancy on any further projects whatsoever. The relationship was ruined, and the client completely lost.

It is likely that none of these consultants was technically incompetent and certain that those who upset their client did not intend to do so. Technical competence is not sufficient by itself; the client relationship has to be actively managed, and this is the topic of this chapter.

WHY THE CLIENT RELATIONSHIP IS IMPORTANT

A good client relationship yields considerably more benefits than simply the esteem of a satisfied client. Quite apart from the fact that it is easier and more pleasant to do business with a satisfied client, there are clear commercial advantages.

Strategic benefits

Products and services can be based on the spectrum shown in Figure 9.1. At one end you have unique products; a famous painting might fall into this category.

Fairly close to that end must be the monopoly suppliers of a product. At the other end are commodity products – those that change very little according to the supplier, and for which there are many suppliers. Food retailing is an example of this: there is no difference in a particular brand of soap powder depending on the shop you buy it at.

Plainly, a salesperson is in a lot stronger position when a product lies towards the left-hand side of the spectrum. The purpose of branding a product is to move from the right-hand side towards the left, by giving attributes to the product additional to the qualities of the product itself. At the simplest level this might be attractive packaging; in the service industry it is achieved by reputation and fashion.

From a client's point of view, the services offered by a consultancy firm are really undifferentiated products; how the services are delivered is therefore fundamental in creating a good reputation. The quality of a consultant's reputation is vital in getting new business. Positive recommendations from satisfied clients to others in their network are worth many hours of selling and marketing by the consultant. Conversely, there is much truth in the old adage 'One bad job costs a hundred good ones.'

A good relationship helps sales

As has been already noted, former clients are perhaps the best source of further business – either by asking the consultant to continue to provide services in a particular area of specialization or by giving the consultancy practice the opportunity to provide a wider range of services.

Conversely, few consultants can claim to have an invulnerable client base. Just as they will seek to enlarge the size of their businesses by acquiring the clients of their competitors, so too will their competitors themselves be attempting to do the same. A poor client relationship will make a client more open to an approach from a competing consultancy practice for future work.

The client relationship must be actively managed

It is tempting to believe that the quality of client relationships is simply the result of luck or happenstance. This is not true. The client relationship must be actively managed in a way complementary to the technical work being carried out by the consultant. Consultants must bring competence to both these tasks if they are to be truly effective.

Consultants have taken up their specialization because of their interest in the topic. Their training is directed towards achieving excellence in the technical aspects of their work. But the judgement made by clients about the quality of a consultant will not be simply on the technical aspects of their work together; it will also depend on a variety of other factors that contribute to the nature of their mutual relationship. For example, the consultant who carries out a project to a high standard but takes too long over it will leave a trail of discontented clients.

Client relationships rarely deteriorate because consultants think them unimportant or are personally insensitive. It is that the task of active client relationship management can often too easily be crowded out by other activities until some (avoidable) crisis arises, which brings it forcibly to the consultant's attention.

ACCOUNT MANAGEMENT

Most business comes from existing clients. The process by which a consultancy engages with existing or past clients – whether or not you are currently conducting any work for them – is how I define 'account management', the second element of Figure 3.1 in Chapter 3. The task of account management may be undertaken by consultants alongside other tasks; in some practices, it may be their principal task. In what follows I shall refer to all as 'account managers'.

Account management is an activity that is ongoing irrespective of whether or not the consultancy practice is engaged in a project with a client. The task of the account manager is to maintain the relationship and to see that both client and consultancy extract value from it. For example, the account manager should know of the client's relevant priorities and be in a position to offer relevant consultancy help, should it be required. Referring back to Figure 4.4 in Chapter 4 (Prospection: The EDIT process) you will see that expressions of interest arise from both client initiated and consultant developed opportunities. It is the job of the account manager to facilitate both of these. The allocation of clients to account managers will probably be based on market segmentation.

Market segmentation and account management

The need for consultancy services and the manner in which they are sold varies according to segment and therefore it makes sense

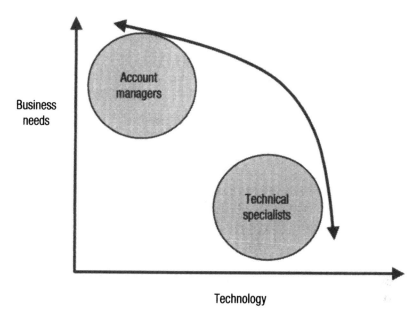

Figure 9.2   The role of the account manager

to allocate clients of similar kinds to the same account manager. The types of segmentation that consultancies use include:

● geographic;

● market sector;

● consultancy service or product.

This segmentation often provides the basis on which the consultancy practice is organized. Thus, a large consultancy may have a London office (geographic segmentation) in which there are specialists marketing IT consultancy services (consultancy service segmentation) to national government bodies (market sector). On the other hand, a sole practitioner may market his or her services in a specialist area of consultancy across the United Kingdom, irrespective of sector.

The task of the account manager

An essential process in managing a consultancy firm is illustrated in Figure 9.2.

The technological capabilities of a consultancy practice do not readily map on to the business needs of organizations. There needs to be a translation process between the two so that the know-how of consultancy firms can be deployed to best effect within the client organization and the consultancy firm gathers intelligence on the emerging needs of its client marketplace.

Located in the diagram are technical specialists and account managers. Technical specialists will have a deep understanding of their specialization and its application, often within a market sector or set of circumstances. In this capacity they will not have a similar depth of knowledge of specific client organizations as account managers. For account managers, the reverse will be true. They will be very close to their client organizations, and have a major responsibility for mediating the connection between business needs and consulting technology.

Performance of the account manager task

The account manager has a major role in promoting the competitiveness of a consultancy firm. Referring back to Figure 9.1, it is worth reflecting where, in a given product-market sector, competitive advantage lies in consultancy. The fact is that the quality of individual consultants is broadly similar (and there is a certain amount of movement between firms). The offerings are also similar, addressing as they do, common predicaments in organizations that are broadly similar. The methodologies, however, to reach the desired outcomes may vary from firm to firm. Moreover, the nature of the relationship, how it is conducted and managed, between individuals in the consultancy firm and those in the client, will also vary.

Treacy and Wiersema suggest that competitive advantage lies in changing what customers value and how it is delivered, then boosting the level of value that customers expect (1993). They go on to suggest that companies that have taken leadership positions offer superior customer value in one of three value disciplines, whilst meeting or exceeding standards in the other two. The value disciplines they identify are operational excellence, customer intimacy and product leadership. Of these, the latter two are relevant to the job of the account manager.

Customer intimacy is about fitting the offering to the needs of the customer. This is familiar territory to the consultant; every proposal is – at least in theory – the design of a product tailored to the needs of the client. But the perception of the 'needs of the client' is all-important; to what extent is it current? So a key task of the account manager is to be acutely aware of – perhaps even anticipate – the particular needs of an organization and the executives in it for outside support. As one account manager said to me, 'If the first I hear of something significant at one of my clients is in the press, then I'm not doing my job!'

Product leadership concerns continuous production of state-of-the-art products and services. This is of interest to consultancy firms not only in so far as their own activities are concerned, but also with respect to the needs of their clients. The link between consultancy and client is a two-way street in this respect: the consultancy can contribute to the client's thinking, but so too can the client contribute to the consultancy's.

So, the account manager has an important strategic role as the conduit between consultancy and client. But there is a further important aspect.

Depth of the relationship

We noted above the importance of the relationship in determining competitive position. It also affects the nature of the work that is undertaken. Broadly, the work that consultants do for clients can be divided into two kinds: 1) determining the development agenda; 2) implementing the development agenda. The latter follows from the former. Implementation might be, say, of a particular software application for a business's management information system. The need for this, and indeed for the management information system, will be an aspect of the client's development agenda.

Involvement in formulating the development agenda brings you closer to the heart of the business. Consultants involved in this must of necessity have a close relationship with individual client executives, and have their trust. The corollary is that only those consultants who have this sort of relationship will be allowed by the client to engage in agenda-setting type work. By contrast, implementation is better defined, and is the continuation of the initiatives on the client agenda. If the task is well defined, it becomes more commoditized, and differentiation is less easy.

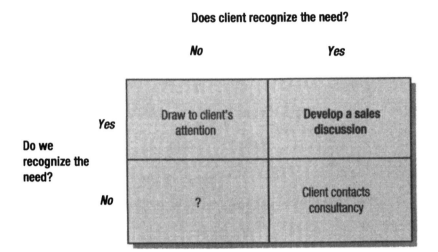

Figure 9.3 The value of maintaining the client relationship

So, the upshot of this logic is that effective account management is a key differentiator. Which is not so earth shattering – we all prefer to do business with people we like and trust.

Maintaining the client relationship in between projects

Although there may be other reasons for networking with a client, the fundamental value derives from the flow of business yielded from investing in the relationship. Already mentioned has been the metaphor of the relationship as a bridge, while sales are the traffic flowing over it: there is no traffic if there is no bridge; but a bridge is of little value if it carries no traffic.

The value of maintaining the relationship is illustrated in Figure 9.3. The figure shows different circumstances in which consultancy and client react to the perception of need.

A sales discussion will ensue only if both sides perceive the need, while if neither see a need, nothing will happen. Account management is particularly pertinent to the other circumstances (depicted in the boxes top right and bottom left) where only one of the parties sees the need.

The cheapest form of selling is when the client asks you for help – they contact you because they see a need for your services (box on bottom right). This they will do only if they are aware of what you do and the key task of the account manager, therefore, in this respect is maintaining awareness. The techniques of doing this include promotional activities applicable to finding new clients (see Chapter 4) but in addition, the account manager can maintain contact through visits and meetings with client staff. This also helps to fulfil the requirements of the box top left – both in identifying needs and providing the opportunity to find out whether they are apparent and important to the client.

The state of readiness of a client for a particular project or intervention changes with time. Keeping in contact allows you to check whether a client is now ready for that in which they were not interested a year ago.

FACTORS CONTRIBUTING TO THE QUALITY OF A RELATIONSHIP

For the remainder of this chapter we will be looking at client relationships in the context of a consultancy project. Every consultancy project starts with a fund of goodwill from the client towards the consultant. There is no particular reason under normal circumstances why this should be exhausted during a project – except by mismanagement! So, what a consultant needs to know is the anatomy of client satisfaction (or dissatisfaction), which can be derived from an understanding of the client relationship. The quality of a client relationship will depend on:

- features of the consultancy practice;

- characteristics of the client;

- the consultancy project being undertaken and its effect on the relationship.

Given an understanding of these, a consultant can plan and manage a client relationship to optimize it. The chapter therefore concludes with some suggestions of the skills and activities that will help to create satisfied clients.

Features of the consultancy practice

One reason that client relationships suffer is that there is a natural conflict between the needs of a consultancy practice and those of its clients. This is illustrated in Figure 9.4.

Clients want:	Consultancies want:
The most appropriate consultant	To use who's available
Instant attention	To service a number of clients
To pay only for the time spent on the job	To bill as much time as possible
Experienced consultants	To train inexperienced consultants
	To spread experienced people thinly

Figure 9.4 The different wants of clients and consultancies

This conflict becomes focused on the individual consultant, who is subject to demands from several sources. Consultants often have more than one client, each with their own requirements and seeking a level of service as if each was the only client. The consultant also has duties to his or her own employer and superiors (see Figure 9.5).

Taken together, these demands may present a consultant with a dilemma; does he look after client A or client B first? Does he or she carry out the additional work that he or she knows client C requires, or does he or she take on the more lucrative work of client D? Consultants will also have their own preferences in terms of the type of work they undertake or clients they deal with, which will also influence the choices they make. The skill with which consultants can deal with these conflicting demands has a considerable influence over their ability to manage the client relationship.

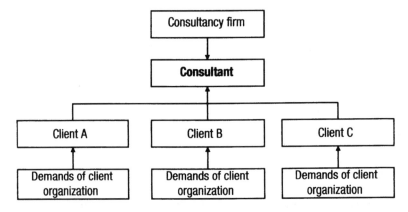

Figure 9.5 Conflicting demands on a consultant

Characteristics of the client

Not only does the consultant have a responsibility for the quality of a client relationship – the client also has a responsibility. This is not simply policing the services being provided by the consultant – it is active cooperation. The relationship between consultant and client should be a partnership, working together towards the same project goals.

The individual with whom the consultant is dealing will also be subject to demands, as shown in Figure 9.5. Sometimes these change and in turn so too do his or her requirements of the consultant. The consultant must be sufficiently flexible to respond to these changes where necessary.

Another important consideration is how well the client uses consultants. Being an employer does not automatically make someone a good manager. Similarly, although the client is paying a fee, this does not make them expert at using consultants.

What makes for a good client? Eve Bingham, writing in *Management Consultancy* magazine cited the following, based on her research. 'Good clients bring to [the] relationship:

- a clear picture of desired results, but not how to achieve them;

- a tough, questioning approach to proposals, demanding to see how a course of action will deliver;

- a recognition of the importance of feedback, so the consultant constantly learns about results, positive or negative, of their interventions;

- an appreciation that it needs time to build a relationship by keeping in touch, taking time to explore the brief and encourage questions, to review feedback and to redesign the project if necessary;

- a sensitivity to the importance of acknowledging a positive contribution: the ability to say thank you.'

Helping the client become a good client

In recent years, more attention has been paid to the skills of being a good client. The Institute of Management Consultancy sponsors a Client User Group, which has studied the characteristics of a good client. These are being updated continuously, and so refer to the Institute's Web site (www.imc.co.uk) for the most recent thinking on the topic.

Not all clients, sadly, exhibit these characteristics, so one of the tasks of consultants is to help their clients to become good clients. After all, if the client has never used consultants before, there is no reason why they should be able to use them well. And, even if they have used them, they may be misguided. So here are three, contradictory, precepts to remember in dealing with clients:

- *The client is always wrong.* The popular adage is, of course, 'The customer is always right.' This cannot – must not – be the case in consultancy, where the consultant's role is to take a view independent of the client. You should therefore question the assumptions, objectives and constraints set by clients and ask, 'Are these appropriate?'

- *The client is often right.* Having done the questioning above, the consultant will often come to this conclusion, but there is more to this precept. Sometimes it can be easy as a consultant to develop a mind-set that clients are misguided incompetents, who can do nothing without the help of a consultant. So you need to be aware of the strengths of a client's thinking and decisions as well as the weaknesses.

- *Sell them what they need in terms of what they want!* This is well worth repeating. Occasionally there may be a need for confrontation, but the rest of the time – go with the flow. In this sense, dealing with clients is like the art of judo. In judo, skill lies not in opposing your opponent but in directing their energy so that they throw themselves. The art in dealing with clients is to direct their energies so that they move in the desired direction. A technique for doing this is to start in their preferred direction, but to educate them by use of data feedback so they start to look at things differently and move in a more appropriate direction.

The effect of the project on the client relationship

A consultancy project will affect the client relationship not just in terms of its technical quality, but also through the quality of project

Figure 9.6 Perceptions are all

performance and the quality of the personal relationship between client staff and consultant. Figure 9.6 shows the key elements in each of these.

The quality of project performance

It is rarely the technical quality of a project that leads to client dissatisfaction; clients are more interested in ends than means. The key aspect of a project that influences a client relationship is therefore deliverables – what the consultant is to provide to the client. It is for these that the client has engaged and will pay the consultant. The timing of deliverables is also crucial; clients get upset when deliverables are behind schedule.

Methods are the means used to create the deliverables. Problems arise with methods when there is disagreement about the details, or which of the consultant or client was meant to carry out a particular task. Every consultant activity has an impact on the client system. Problems can also occur therefore when a project has an unwelcome effect on the client. It is a rare project that does not involve some client participation, so it is important to be clear about who should be involved and how they should be involved.

The basis of reporting to the client should also be clear; clients become irritated when they do not feel adequately informed. So this applies to progress reports as well as assignment reports.

The quality of interpersonal relationships

As already mentioned, it is reasonable to assume that at the start of an assignment the consultant team begins with a fund of goodwill from the client. So the aim must be at least to avoid disappointing the client and, preferably, to improve the client's view of the consultants.

As the relationship is between individuals, the quality of the interpersonal relationship between the consultant and the client's staff will have an effect on the total relationship. The important factors are shown in Figure 9.6.

The needs of the client must be considered, both in terms of the project and how it is to contribute to the client's personal objectives. Problems occur if a consultant does not discern a client's real needs. Sometimes a client might have a hidden agenda, either as a principal or ancillary objective of the project. (Usually these agendas are political in nature!)

If clients' expectations are not met they will be disappointed and relationships will suffer. You must therefore take care to manage the client's expectations so that they can be met. These expectations relate not only to the project but also to you yourself, for instance, in the way in which you conduct yourself. For example, if you are working on client premises, the client may have firm expectations about:

- what time you should arrive and leave;

- whether you can spend time on the telephone on business other than that to do with the project in hand;

- style of dress;

- your access to people in other departments or at more senior levels;

- the degree of formality in your relationship with client staff.

Infringing these expectations can have just as serious repercussions on the consultant/client relationship as failing to meet the formal terms of reference. Consequently, many consultants use the period of familiarization at the start of an assignment to collect data on the 'code of conduct' they are to follow within the client organization. In a similar way, you can have quite legitimate expectations of a client. You can reasonably expect the client:

- to be accessible;

- to provide the resources promised;

- to cooperate in the execution of the project;

- to be supportive of the project;

- to tell you of changes of circumstances that may influence the project;

- to discuss any concerns or apprehensions about how the project is proceeding.

Although these are all the responsibilities of the client, you should monitor that they are being provided. If they are not, it is your job, as the expert, to alert the client to any difficulties and advise on how they should be resolved.

How the client and consultant view each other will depend on the other items already mentioned. That relationship will in part be a self-fulfilling prophecy; a client who loses confidence in a consultant will be far more difficult to satisfy.

Occasionally you find that there is conflict between a client and a consultant, or among members of client staff. A good diagnostic rule in analysing conflict is to remember the sequence:

1. goals;

2. roles;

3. procedures;

4. personal animosity.

What this sequence suggests is that if you do run into conflict, do not assume it is necessarily a matter of personal animosity – there are other possible causes, which are shown in the order of the list above. The easy way to remember the sequence is to imagine two people undertaking a car journey, who are arguing. They will argue if:

1. They have not agreed on where they are going (goals).

2. Although they have agreed where they are going, they have not agreed who is to drive (roles).

3. Although they have agreed on where they are going and who is going to drive, they have not decided the route they are to take (procedures).

If, after agreement on all these points, they are still arguing, then perhaps it can be put down to personal animosity!

Perceptions are all

Also illustrated in Figure 9.6 is that all the transactions between consultant and client are viewed through their respective perceptions. It is not 'objective reality' that matters but how you each see things. The client's opinion will be affected by how he or she evaluates progress on the project compared with the promises you have made and the impression the client has of the overall professionalism of the practice.

The former is about communications and expectations. A key job for a consultant in managing client relationships is to reassure the client that the project is proceeding satisfactorily. This means not only communicating progress, but also ensuring that the client's expectations accord with those of the consultant. For example, returning to the ICC case study in Chapter 6, John Smith may embark on a project to study alternative methods of producing cutlery, and in doing so, he might choose to discuss the pros and cons of present methods with the operatives at ICC. If, however, the General Manager's view is that there should be no consultation, there is a mismatch of expectations. Keeping the client informed is not just about reporting the past but also managing his or her expectations for the future.

The impression of the professionalism of a consultancy practice depends on the administrative as well as professional staff. The client comes into contact with switchboard and secretarial staff, receptionists, and with accounts people in respect of invoices. Most contacts will be fleeting and will not be face to face, but all will contribute to the client's impression of the practice. Many professional practices have therefore trained all their staff in key aspects in delivering good client care.

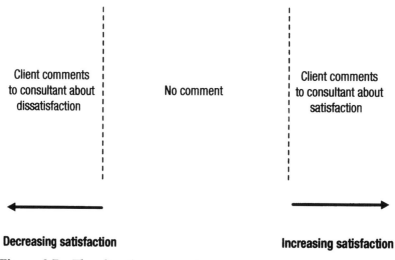

Figure 9.7   The client's comments

MONITORING THE CLIENT RELATIONSHIP

Remember clients will always have a view of the consultant, but whether they tell the consultant of their view is another matter. This is illustrated in Figure 9.7.

Note that there is on both sides a threshold of dissatisfaction or satisfaction that must be reached before the client will comment. The consultant's aim must be continuing positive satisfaction, rather than simply assuming that no feedback means that the client is satisfied. There are two things that the consultant must do to address this: 1) monitor the quality of the client relationship by actively soliciting feedback and 2) adopt good practices in operating consultancy projects, so that the risk of client dissatisfaction is reduced.

Regular progress reviews enable the client to feed back concerns, and can be used to manage expectations. Even so, there is a danger that the consultant does not hear what the client is saying; you have to listen carefully to hear softly voiced criticisms.

Handling complaints

Inevitably from time to time a client may complain about progress or the way a job is being run, or the impact of it on client staff. Do

not overreact to complaints – they might not be justified or could
be totally unfounded. Indeed, a complaint is valuable, as it means
that the client cares enough to tell you. A complaint enables you to
put things right, or to improve service. If the client does not tell
you, you cannot put things right.

Here is an effective way of handling a complaint from a client:

1. Thank them for bringing it to your notice and giving you a
    chance to put it right. (Far better this way than that they should
    simply get annoyed, leaving the matter unresolved.) Tell them
    you're sorry they have been upset, but don't apologize for hav-
    ing done something wrong. (You don't even know if it's your
    fault at this stage, but you can regret their being upset.)

2. Encourage them to give you the full story and note the details.
    Don't interrupt while the client is giving vent to their feelings
    and don't argue, however justified you think you may be in
    doing so – this will only make them more irritated.

3. When you have all the information, check whether the complaint
    is founded. Sometimes difficulties arise from misunderstandings
    and a simple explanation will sort things out. If you cannot
    deal with the complaint at this meeting, however, explain this
    and tell the client what you plan to do. In particular, agree
    when you will get back to them with a response and make sure
    you do follow up.

A critical test of any provider of goods or services is how they handle complaints. If a complaint is handled professionally and well,
it can strengthen rather than weaken the client relationship. There
are sound reasons for this. Complaints usually arise because a
client has a problem and when you work with a client to resolve a
complaint you are, in effect, engaged in joint problem solving. Joint
problem solving strengthens relationships; indeed, it is a mechanism often used in team building programmes. So, a capably
resolved complaint can strengthen the relationship.

It is important to know when to call for help when dealing with
a complaint. This is particularly necessary when a complaint is
about you (when you are not in the best position to resolve it) or if
the client is seeking some commercial compensation. Sometimes
things do go wrong (no consultant is perfect!) but do not compound
the mistake by not asking for help when you need it.

CREATING SATISFIED CLIENTS

The comments thus far in this chapter have been so defensive, focusing on how to avoid a poor client relati ᵤp. The remainder of this chapter looks at the other side of the coin – how to carry out consultancy projects so that clients are positively satisfied rather than simply 'not dissatisfied'. This starts with the planning of the project, continues throughout the delivery and finishes with its completion.

Setting up the project

Clear and comprehensive terms of reference and terms of business are the foundation of a good client relationship (see Chapters 7 and 8). If you did not sell the assignment, but are operating a project sold by someone else, then you should check that the points below have been covered; if they are not, you must clarify them right at the start of the project:

- the scope of the project;
- the deliverables to the client;
- the method by which you will carry out the project;
- the programme of work involved;
- the resources required, including the support you expect from the client;
- the fees you are charging and when they become payable;
- when the project is to be complete.

You also need to know something of the sponsor, particularly their attitude to the project. What are the payoffs for him or her if the project is successful – what will they get out of it? How used are they to using outside advice? If a client has not used consultants before, they may need help in using your services to best effect.

Planning the project

With any project other than the most trivial, it will be necessary to have review or reporting points with the client during its course. Progress reviews should take place at a regular frequency (for example, once per week or per month) or at milestones – points in the project where a major phase or stage is complete. Progress reviews can do much to reassure a client that a project is proceeding well and build confidence in the consultant. The converse – not keeping a client informed – can result in their feeling out of control or vulnerable, even if there is no basis for this.

When making your project plan, try to build in some slack so that you have some flexibility to accommodate delays. If your planning is such that any change in circumstances means that you will fail to meet targets, inevitably this will happen.

During the project

There are several things you can do that will enable you to develop a good client relationship during a project:

- *Build confidence during the early stages.* Every project should start well; after all, you would not have won the contract if the client did not have the confidence that you were the best firm for the job. But during the early stages, even established clients will be checking out the firm's credentials, to see if that first impression was correct. Early in a project it is particularly important, therefore, to build a client's confidence. Being prompt and prepared at all client meetings, perhaps having them more frequently than you might otherwise have, will help; so too will a businesslike approach and achieving all the initial targets required on time. One particularly good way of building confidence at the early stages is the 'quick success' – achieving a result or delivering value beyond that expected.

- *Add value.* The 'quick success' formula will work throughout a project, so try to add value by doing more than the client expects. This does not mean providing free services, but look for opportunities of giving extra benefits from your work or help that may be beyond your brief. The most commercially advantageous to you are those that are valuable to a client but cheap for you to provide. A simple example is giving a client a publication or report from the consultancy practice on a topic of concern to him or her.

- *Publicize good news.* Make sure the client knows about all the successes you have achieved in your project. This can be done via progress reviews, but also make sure you can bring them up during casual conversations with client staff. If you are really sophisticated you will plan 'sound bites' so that you have a snappy response to the query, 'How is it going?' Your sound bite should consist of a 'newsworthy' comment about how the project is progressing. These items can be passed on by client staff. Remember that your client will want to reassure his or her colleagues that the project is proceeding successfully.

- *Dealing with bad news.* If something goes wrong that can be easily remedied without concerning the client, there is no need to bother him or her. If the client has to be informed, then it is better to do so before the problem becomes a crisis. Ideally you should go to the client with a statement of the problem and how you propose to solve it. Sometimes, however, you may need to work together to resolve the problem. Often clients will put in extra effort to solve the problem or mitigate its effect on their organization to save their own credibility with their colleagues.

Personal skills of the consultant

There are personal skills that make it easier for consultants to manage client relationships well. These are as follows.

Manage your time effectively

Time is the consultant's stock in trade; it is the commodity that you are selling. Time is also a consultant's scarcest resource, so it must be managed carefully. This requires three important skills:

- Establishing and working to a set of priorities.

- Giving sufficient time to existing commitments.

- Learning to say 'No'. Contrary to popular belief, there are a limited number of hours per day that a consultant can work at optimal performance. There comes a point when a consultant has to say 'No' to the demands of a practice or the client.

Position yourself correctly

Consultants must position themselves so that they are the equal of the client – at whatever level the client in the organization is. In particular, the consultant should make clear the right to say 'No' to a client, for example when they have unreasonable fee or time-scale expectations.

Handling conflicting demands

It may not be within the consultant's power to resolve a conflict of demands between a client and the consultancy practice. This is particularly difficult for junior consultants, who could find themselves in a 'no win' situation – they will upset someone whatever they do. They should seek the help of a more senior consultant – their boss – to resolve it.

When things go wrong, deal with them

Inevitably there will be occasions when things go wrong at either the project or personal level between consultant and client. When this happens, it should be recognized as a problem and dealt with as such. It is the way a consultant deals with problems that is a key test of how good he or she is at managing the client relationship. Young consultants are frequently reluctant to admit to mistakes that they cannot deal with; far better to admit them, however, before they turn into crises.

Don't knock anybody

It is rarely to a consultant's credit to criticize his colleagues, his clients or his competitors to his client. Where a client has a justifiable complaint about a consultant colleague, the consultant should acknowledge and deal with it rather than denigrating the colleague.

Be attentive

A lot of effort goes into wooing the client for business. Once the business has been secured, the client will still expect attentive service. In practice this means that the consultant must be accessible to his clients and give them prompt attention. Equally, the consultant must be able to avoid the 'time wasters' without losing them as clients.

The end of the project

I am told that in one European country there is the phrase, 'To say goodbye like an Englishman', which means to go without saying goodbye! The best source of further work and referrals to new clients is past clients, and so every project should be concluded with this in mind. The project should be signed off from both sides – the consultancy's and the client's. There should be a clear agreement on the successful completion of the project and perhaps an exchange of letters confirming the client's satisfaction. Astute consultants will make sure that warm letters of praise from clients are passed on to their own superiors.

References

Beckhard, R (1989) 'A model for the executive management of transformational change', in *The 1989 Annual: Developing Human Resources*, University Associates

Bingham, E (1992) 'It takes two to tango', *Management Consultancy*, April

Handy, C (1989) *The Age of Unreason*, Business Books Ltd

Majaro, Simon (1988) *The Creative Gap*, Longman

Markham, C (2003) *Practical Management Consultancy*, Accountancy Books

Miller, R B and Heiman, S E (1989) *Strategic Selling*, Kogan Page

von Oech, R (1990) *A Whack on the Side of the Head*, Thorsons Publishing Group

Treacy, M and Wiersema, F (1993) 'Customer intimacy and other value disciplines', *Harvard Business Review*, January–February

Wittreich, W J (1966) 'How to buy/sell professional services', *Harvard Business Review*, March–April

Index

Printed in Great Britain
by Amazon